CW00823263

In from the Cuithes

An Orkney Anthology

In from the Cuithes

An Orkney Anthology

Edited by Howie Firth

THE
ORKNEY
PRESS

Published by The Orkney Press Ltd in 1995
© Contributors severally

All rights reserved
The Orkney Press Ltd
12 Craigiefield Park, St Ola
Kirkwall, Orkney KW15 1TE

Lay-out and typesetting by Birgir Christiansen
in 12 on 13 pt Bembo

Printed in Great Britain by The Orcadian
ISBN 0 907618 40 5

Cover photograph by Keith Allardyce

The publishers wish to acknowledge the excellent work of
the art pupils of Kirkwall Grammar School in creating
illustrations and drawings for this book. The pupils' names
and the pages where their work appears are listed below:

Secondary 2 Art Class: Dean Adams 17, Kenny Scott 19, Robert
Lamont 23, Angela Kirkpatrick 26, Anna Laughton 36, Ryan
Craigie 41, Sarah Glue 50, Adam Stanger 58, Christine
Hourston 62, Claire Logie 67, Robert Lamont 72, Matthew
Drever 75, Karen Aim 80, Keith Rosie 85, Simon Varley 88,
William Mackay 113, Isla Rae Shortland 127, Claire Logie
129, Aaron Rendall 148, Ian Johnston 154, Gerry Tait 160,
Laura Cromarty 166, Karen Graham 170.

Secondary 6 Art Class: Claire Budge 10 and 63, Amy Girvan
139, Karen Laird 162.

CONTENTS

Introduction *Howie Firth*   7
Orkney: A Ferrylouper's View *Gerald G. A. Meyer*   11
The Orkney Character *Ronald Miller*   15
Before We Roonded Hoy *David Towers*   18
Autumn in Orkney *Eddie Balfour*   20
Rackwick Bay *Hazel Parkins*   22
Pictures from the Wind *David Hutchison*   24
The Island Climate *Rev. George Low*   27
Aurora *George Mackay Brown*   29
The West in Wind and Sun *Bessie Skea*   30
Living by the Sea *Elaine R. Bullard*   35
Eynhallow *John Mooney*   37
The Storm *Eric Linklater*   42
A Nature Miscellany *Hugh Marwick*   46
The German Fleet in Scapa Flow *Cmdr. Yorck von Reuter*   51
König *Peter L. Smith*   53
With the Lighthouse Yacht in Orkney *Sir Walter Scott*   59
All at Sea *Bryce Wilson*   61
Growing up with the Sea *Capt. Robert L. Sutherland*   64
Stromness – 70 Years Ago *Jackie Brown*   68
'Puffer' *George S. Robertson*   73
Boots Shoes & Bends *Fiona MacInnes*   76
Memories of Robert Shaw *Archie Bevan*   78
Necessary Magic *Morag McGill*   81
Sillocks and Cuithes *Capt. John Gray*   86
Summer Sounds in Stronsay *Tom McLachlan*   89
Duel on the Fairway *R. T. Johnston*   92
Memories of Jo Grimond *Howie Firth*   107
Entering Parliament *Jo Grimond*   109

Laura Grimond *Howie Firth*   114
Some Orkney Artists *Jo Grimond*   119
Stanley Cursiter – A Stromness Neighbour *Howie Firth* 122
Billy Peace the Provost's Dog *Stanley Cursiter*   124
Hint of Foreign Parts in Kirkwall *Rhoda Spence*   128
Voices of St Magnus Cathedral *Ernest R. Marwick*   130
The Blacksmith's Shop *Freddie Gibson*   133
The Shoemaker in Kirkwall *Jimmy Harrison*   137
Stories behind the Ba' *Gordon Linklater*   140
Uppies and Doonies *John D. M. Robertson*   145
Twenty Doonies in the Basin *David Horne*   149
Feast Days *John Firth*   155
Echoes of Hogmanay *John Goar*   159
Wine, Women & Song *Margaret Headley*   161
Hogmanay and New Year *George Mackay Brown*   165
Christmas in Wartime *Marjorie Linklater*   167
Willick and the Christmas Repast *David Sinclair*   171
Ballad Hunting in the Orkney Islands *Otto Andersson*   178
Dancing in Flotta *Dr Tom Flett*   184
Married in Rousay *Maggie Ann Clouston*   188
Orkney Weddings *Walter Traill Dennison*   190
Wanted: One Red Flag *John D. Mackay*   194
Harvest *William Smith*   196
Thrashing *James Omond*   197
Mansie's Threshing *Robert Rendall*   198
In the But-Hoose *James Omond*   202
Wer New Byre *Minnie Russell*   203
Saving Time in Shapinsay *A. J. Firth*   204
The *Iona* *Bill Dennison*   208
A Painted Ship *J. A. Rousay*   212
The Driftwood Fiddle *Harry Berry*   222
Requiescant *William Groundwater*   226
Laura Meets a Traveller *Mary Brunton*   228
A Letter from North Ronaldsay *Ian Scott*   231
Remembering George Corrigall *Mary Bichan*   235
Strolling up the Lyde *George Corrigall*   237
The Approach of Winter *Elaine R. Bullard*   239
Merlin *Edwin Muir*   240

INTRODUCTION

I think there are at least four reasons why Orkney has produced so many good writers.

First of all, Orcadians are highly social. Edwin Muir rightly said that in Orkney the lives of living men turn into legend. Out of the lives of so many colourful characters there are stories and comments, to be joyfully savoured and retold.

Next, Orcadians are craftsmen, in an island where resources are often limited, and a piece of driftwood can become a lintel or a fiddle. They tend to use words in the way of a craftsman, carefully putting together a structured account, whether in a ship's log or a memory of a bygone time.

Also, Orcadians love reading and admire education. The long winters are a factor, but there is a real joy in learning about the world, and understanding the deeper reasons for its patterns.

And fourthly, Orcadians are explorers. It was once economic necessity, but there is a delight in setting off on a journey of discovery. Through the centuries Orcadians have welcomed the world's travellers, and had their own appetite for travel whetted. I think that the great Orcadian writers are explorers, whose stamina and vision seems to grow with age, to take them ever further into unknown lands that are a natural home.

This book is an attempt to give a flavour of the range of writing Orkney produces. The sources are varied. There are extracts from books and magazines and newspapers and talks and radio programmes, and even a song or two. I have tried to choose pieces which fit together and flow along in a sequence, so that one item can often give a context to the next. I have abridged sometimes where necessary, to help to focus selections within the space available. For the same reason, I have in some cases also made some slight adjustments to paragraphing or punctuation.

The quality of writing to choose from is such that I have had to omit many items, among them some particular favourites. I had in the end to recognise that I had to start somewhere, and I hope to make amends for the gaps on a future occasion.

To set the scene, I have written short introductions to the various selections, and for the same reason have included three longer biographical items that I have written previously.

As well as material already published, I have taken the opportunity to seek out new contributions. The response has been excellent. Various people have been stimulated to write down memories of previous times, and a number of highly promising writers of a new generation have produced some exciting material.

Orkney writers of all ages do need encouragement, because amongst our many virtues as a community there is also our reluctance at times to recognise the full ability of fellow-Orcadians. There are some very good writers in Orkney, who have the skills to go very far; they need a climate in which they can believe in themselves and commit themselves.

A further pleasure has been the opportunity to demonstrate the quality of Orkney's young artists through the delightful illustrations by pupils of Kirkwall Grammar School.

A book of this sort is only possible through much help from many people, who write items, trace sources, make material available, give permissions, and generally make the anthologiser's task a happy one. Particular thanks go to Bobby Leslie at Orkney Library and Alison Fraser at the Library Archives, John Fergusson and Kathryn Gourlay at BBC Radio Orkney, the staff of *The Orcadian*, and Keith Laird at Kirkwall Grammar School.

Finally, the title. Gathering material for a book like this is a bit like sifting the waters for fish, after which you set off home to enjoy it. It was also the title I once used for a student revue, and it seemed a pity to let it lie when it could be used again. I've found much pleasure in the work of the various writers who are in this book, and I hope you do too.

Howie Firth
October 1995

ACKNOWLEDGMENTS

The following appear by kind permission of the author:
'Orkney: A Ferrylouper's View' by Gerald G. A. Meyer, 'Rackwick Bay' by Hazel Parkins, 'Pictures from the Wind' by David Hutchison, 'The West in Wind and Sun' by Bessie Skea, 'Living by the Sea' by Elaine R. Bullard, 'The German Fleet in Scapa Flow' by Cmdr. Yorck von Reuter, '*König*' by Peter L. Smith, 'All at Sea' by Bryce Wilson, 'Growing up with the Sea' by Capt. Robert L. Sutherland, 'Stromness – 70 Years ago' by Jackie Brown, 'Boots Shoes & Bends' by Fiona MacInnes, 'Memories of Robert Shaw' by Archie Bevan, 'Necessary Magic' by Morag McGill, 'Sillocks and Cuithes' by Capt. John Gray, 'The Blacksmith's Shop' by Freddie Gibson, 'Stories behind the Ba' by Gordon Linklater, 'Uppies and Doonies' by John D. M. Robertson, 'Wine, Women & Song' by Margaret Headley, 'Christmas in Wartime' by Marjorie Linklater, 'Willick and the Christmas Repast' by David Sinclair, 'Wer New Byre' by Minnie Russell, 'Saving Time in Shapinsay' by A. J. Firth, 'The *Iona*' by Bill Dennison, 'A Painted Ship' by J. A. Rousay, 'A Letter from North Ronaldsay' by Ian Scott, 'Remembering George Corrigall' by Mary Bichan, 'The Approach of Winter' by Elaine R. Bullard.

The copyright and manuscript holders are thanked for the following contributions: 'The Orkney Character' by Ronald Miller, by kind permission of Mr John Miller; 'Before We Roonded Hoy' by David Towers, by kind permission of Mrs Jean Work; 'Autumn in Orkney' by Eddie Balfour, by kind permission of Mrs R. Balfour; 'Aurora' by George Mackay Brown, by kind permission of the author and John Murray Ltd; 'The Storm' by Eric Linklater, by kind permission of The estate of Eric Linklater; 'Summer Sounds in Stronsay' by Tom McLachlan, by kind permission of Mrs Naismi Flett and *The Orcadian*; 'Duel on the Fairway' by R. T. Johnston, by kind permission of the Johnston family per Mr Ian Bruce; 'Entering Parliament' and 'Some Orkney Artists' by Jo Grimond, by kind permission of the Grimond family per Mr Magnus Grimond; 'Billy Peace the Provost's Dog' by Stanley Cursiter, by kind permission of Mrs Margaret C. Hunter and Orkney Sound Archive; 'Hint of Foreign Parts in Kirkwall' by Rhoda Spence, by kind permission of Mr M. H. Beattie; 'Voices of St Magnus Cathedral' by Ernest R. Marwick, by kind permission of Mr John D. M. Robertson; 'Twenty Doonies in the Basin' by David Horne, by kind permission of Mrs Kim Foden of Herald Printshop; 'Echoes of Hogmanay' by John Goar, by kind permission of Mr John Goar; 'Hogmanay and New Year' by George Mackay Brown, by kind permission of the author and Mrs Kim Foden of Herald Printshop; 'Dancing in Flotta' by kind permission of Mrs Kim Foden of Herald Printshop; 'Wanted: One Red Flag' by John D. Mackay by kind permission of *The Orcadian*; 'Harvest' by William Smith, by kind permission of *The Orcadian*; 'Mansie's Threshing' by Robert Rendall, by kind permission of Mr R. P. Rendall; 'Requiescant' by William Groundwater, by kind permission of Mr Bill Groundwater; 'Merlin' by Edwin Muir, by kind permission of Faber & Faber Ltd.

In some cases where copyright-holders have proved difficult to trace or may have been omitted in error, the publishers wish to apologise for any inconvenience caused, and will be glad to hear from the appropriate parties, so that details can be put on record for the future.

ORKNEY:
A FERRYLOUPER'S VIEW

GERALD G. A. MEYER

(Gerry Meyer came from London to Orkney on an October day in 1940, and within months his previous civilian background in journalism had led Eric Linklater to recruit him as editor for the Forces' wartime newspaper, The Orkney Blast. Gerry went on in peacetime to edit The Orcadian from 1947 until his retirement in 1983, combining professionalism with a mature judgment and a deep feeling for the islands and their wellbeing. He still likes to refer to himself cheerfully as 'a ferrylouper' and to philosophise accordingly – as here in The Scots Magazine in 1969 – about the community to which he has committed himself so affectionately.)

Here in Orkney you are never far from the elements, and from a certain understanding of the human condition. The Orcadian is phlegmatic, easy-going and extremely tolerant. He accepts with philosophic detachment not only his climate but also ferryloupers, who, like me, have come and settled in his midst. He is not easily riled. But woe to you, if not island-born, if you dare hazard any remark about the climate. To the Orkneyman this subject is his preserve and almost sacrosanct, not to be lightly indulged in, even less to be bandied about by a mere ferrylouper.

The greatest compliment a true Orcadian can pay the weather is to describe it as 'no so bad,' and invariably he does so, even on the coldest and greyest of days. If, in all innocence you, a ferrylouper, should happen to remark that it is a bad morning, your Orkney friend will look at you with a pained expression and slowly deliver himself of such a comment as, 'It's worse Sooth.' This is usually followed by an impressive catalogue of the meteorological woes that have afflicted other parts of Britain. You will then realise the tender spot you have touched.

So that now, if any Orcadian ever vouchsafes, as it is his own inalienable right to do so, that it is cold, I quote him the Arctic temperatures recorded by the latest expedition to Spitzbergen; if he mentions rain, I give him the annual rainfall for Fort William, and if he should suggest a haar I recall the London smog. In this way honour is satisfied all round.

It has been said that Orkney has no climate – only samples of weather. And very often these samples leave absolutely nothing to be desired. The islands do have their very beautiful days, in winter as well as summer. I have had visitors from the Continent spending a whole fortnight here with not a drop of rain, who have returned home raving about our weather. In Orkney you must always be prepared for the unexpected.

The air is clear and crystalline, and what enraptured me right from the start was those unforgettable sunrises and sunsets, and those very still, starlit nights with a full moon reflected on the Flow, framed by the silhouette of the gentle Orkney hills. A visitor from Australia once told me that Orkney was the nearest approach he had seen to '3-D.' No wonder that it is the photographer's paradise.

Armed with camera, a favourite occupation of mine during the long summer days, is to climb any one of Orkney's hills. The greatest challenge, of course, is to ascend Hoy's 1565-foot Ward Hill, Orkney's highest, where, on a fine day, you see Fair Isle above the north-eastern horizon, and to the southwards the main peaks of the Northern Highlands.

But it is not necessarily the highest point that gives you the captivating view, as anyone who has been to the top of Brinkie's Brae in Stromness, the Hill of Heddle in Finstown, or Marwick Head, a mile off which Lord Kitchener perished in the *Hampshire* in June 1916, or even Miffia in the parish of Sandwick, will testify.

I remember one particular summer's night finding myself at the summit of Miffia, when, after disturbing countless hares on the way up, and also a pair of golden plover, I exclaimed: 'This is the finest of them all.' The Atlantic surpassed any

Mediterranean blue, and, on the other side, all the lochs of the West Mainland shone like diamonds in their setting of crimson hills. I counted no fewer that seven Orkney lighthouses.

Then there are the stacks, those detached rock pillars, studding Orkney's fretted coast. Most famous of all is the 450-foot Old Man of Hoy, who for centuries has maintained his sphinx-like watch over the turbulent Pentland Firth, and who, at the beginning of the last century stood on two 'feet.' Hitherto unconquered, he was first climbed on July 18, 1966, by Chris Bonington, Rusty Baillie and Tom Patey (of Ullapool). Since then, close on a dozen ascents have been chalked up, one by an eight-year-old boy, accompanied by his father, and another made by the mother of a one-year-old child. How are the mighty fallen!

The Old Man can be seen from only a very few headlands (frequented mainly at week-ends), and because of this, when the sensational rumour went round the island that he had at long last succumbed to the fury of Atlantic seas and winds, it took many hours to establish whether this was true. Eventually, I only elicited the good news that he was still upstanding from the master of the mailboat *St Ola* (Captain J. Stevenson), when his ship berthed at Stromness on her return run from Scrabster. It would have been a sorry day for Orkney had it lost its oldest inhabitant!

Lesser known, but equally imposing stacks, are the 150-foot Yesnaby Castle and North Gaulton Castle (200 feet), both situated on the Mainland's west coast. Top-heavy and pierced at its base by a big hole, Yesnaby is an artist's delight. But, to my mind, North Gaulton, just a mile farther on, and known to only about one in a hundred Orcadians, is the loveliest of them, with its ever-changing aspect as one strolls along the fulmar-frequented cliff-face opposite.

I react differently to each of these fine stacks, and have compared them to Beethoven's symphonies. If the Old Man is the Fifth, a symbol of man triumphant, and Yesnaby the Seventh – surely intriguing North Gaulton, in all its varying moods, is the sprightly Eighth?

Orkney, however, holds other attractions besides hill-climbing, the contemplation of its stacks, bird-watching, the exploration of Skara Brae or Maeshowe, or even of Kirkwall's 800-year-old Cathedral of St Magnus. Most of this has already been well written about.

Orkney is a way of life. It is a communal and as near to a classless society as you can find anywhere. In our little town we all know each other by our Christian names, whether it be the Provost or the driver of the Stromness-Kirkwall bus.

The driver is, in fact, Tommy Drever, who has been on that route for as long as I can remember. To me he is as permanent as the Old Man. Tommy Drever acts as ticket collector, deliverer of messages, and giver of information. On any weekday, there will be found beside his driving seat, before he sets off, an astounding assortment of articles for him to distribute, not only at his destination but at various stages of his 15-mile run between the two towns. He stops here to deliver to a roadside farm a bottle of medicine; a little farther on he halts again to hand somebody else a parcel from the draper. Farther still, he jumps nimbly out of his bus to give a housewife the Sunday joint. On a winter's day, with 5-foot drifts lying around, I don't envy driver Tommy Drever and his multifarious duties.

Yes, it is a closely-integrated society, and yet everyone remains an individual, not wholly absorbed in his own little existence but taking an interest in all the goes on around him – and in the rest of the world. The air and sea do not separate. On the contrary, they are a bridge.

The Scots Magazine, December 1969

THE ORKNEY CHARACTER

RONALD MILLER

(There was a time when Orkney was producing so many brilliant men that the islands' main exports were said to be 'fat cattle and professors.' Many of these distinguished Orcadians found their career embedded them permanently into settlement overseas, but in the case of Professor Ronald Miller, who held the Chair of Geography at Glasgow University for many years, the family connection with Orkney was never broken. After travelling in the course of his life to many places, when he retired it was to the family home in the town of Stromness, where he could grow his tropical plants in his greenhouse and take his boat out to fish off Hoy. He had an almost encyclopaedic knowledge of Orkney, in which the smallest detail such as the type of paint on a boat or the name of a house could be related to the broader picture of island economy and landscape. In short, there was just about no one better suited to reflect on the Orcadian character.)

Life on a small island sets one apart not only literally, but also mentally. Most human beings feel a curious reaction, which cannot be articulated, to living on, or even visiting, a small island. With the exception of the Mainland, none of the islands comprising Orkney is too big for all the inhabitants to know, or know of, all the others. This generates a wonderful sense of community, especially in contrast with a similar-size group set in the continuum of, say, the millions in the English plain. The small population of Orkney – a mere 18,000, less than the combined student total for the universities of Glasgow and Edinburgh – also confers a certain distinctiveness.

But there is also a community of cultural background. There is a general belief that Orcadians are descended from Vikings. However mistaken this may be, it has a unifying effect, though happily not so intoxicating as to lead to the excesses of Up-Helly-Aa. On a more mundane level, the rack-renting lairds of great-grandfather's day inculcated the virtues of hard work and the ability to see a task through, be it ever so distasteful or wearying. Certain other islands of Scotland, with a different background, have been described as placing a high value on leisure. Idleness is not counted a virtue in Orkney. Not that Orcadians are so virtuous: punitive rents, paid in kind, often yielded the laird bad meal (which he exported to Shetland or Norway) and butter so outstandingly foul that it served only to grease carriage wheels. A notable Orcadian of the eighteenth century, James Fea, wrote that Orcadians are 'quick in discerning their interest and indefatigable in the pursuit of it.' Nowadays, presumably, he would say they were go-getters, but he would, we hope, be meaning they were full of get-up-and-go. The Hudson's Bay Company valued Orcadians because they were literate, numerate, docile but tough, conscientious and above all poor, so that they could be engaged for small wages. They also had the reputation of being clannish and reserved. One Orcadian writer called them 'the slyest set of men under the sun.'

In a later generation, another unifying factor appeared. Crippling taxation on big landowners after the 1914-18 war led to the sale of land to its occupiers, and though the average farm was small and all the virtues above were still necessary to remain viable, nearly everyone became a 'peerie laird,' master of all he surveyed up to his boundary fences, and motivated to take advantage of the new and remunerative ideas the government agricultural advisers were offering. Thus while the rest of the country was four-fifths urban, full of wage-earners often doing dull and even meaningless work and building the Bedlam which is our modern industrialised society, Orcadians shared independent owner-occupier status, were self-employed and concerned with real things, the land, the sea, the weather, plants and animals. For a more eloquent expression of this, read George Mackay Brown. They shared, moreover, the same annual cycle of events and work on both land and sea and thus developed a fellowship and almost classless society. As a local man wrote:

> *The solitudes of land and sea assuage*
> *My quenchless thirst for freedom unconfined;*
> *With independent heart and mind*
> *Hold I my heritage.*

But if there is a common background in culture, way of life and standard of values, there is also a unifying influence in the physical environment. Orcadians share in the delights of insularity but deplore in chorus the high cost of transport. They delight in the high summer weather, the simmer dim, the pure crystal-clear air off the sea, the sky full of larks and the scent of clover and meadow-sweet, and they respect each other for the phlegm with which they endure the purgatory which is the winter weather. A deep fellow-feeling is generated by recollections of how sea-sick they have all been in the mail-boat.

The People of Orkney (1986)

BEFORE WE ROONDED HOY

DAVID TOWERS

(David Towers was one of Orkney's most talented entertainers. He wrote and sang his own songs, breaking off from time to time to elaborate in a short monologue, and delighted audiences time and again. He did it all with an impeccable timing which built up to one height after another. He would come out with a comment, and there would be laughter; then a pause, precisely timed; then another comment, even funnier; and after another pause, the punchline, received by a gale of applause and laughter. He lived in Harray, in the very heart of Orkney's farming land, and he worked on the roads for the County Council, which provided the inspiration for songs about working 'in my little yellow oilskin on the County water scheme.' Here, to the tune of 'A Wild Colonial Boy' is another of the classics.)

Doon Sooth across the Pentland Firth's a place I'd never been,
A river or a railway train a thing I'd never seen.
So holidays when neeps were done I sowt f'ae me employ –
I caught the mailboat at the pier, and soon wis roondan Hoy.

It wis the most excitan morn I've spent in a' me life;
I'll no be so excited on the day I tak a wife.
Twa haddocks newly frae the sea – a breakfast I enjoy –
But baith got back intae the sea, before we roonded Hoy.

I needed no alarms that day, tae get me doon the stair,
I whistled like a mavis, while I washed and combed me hair,
Got on me sark and spotted tie, and the suit I bowt frae Croy,
But – feth, I lost me Bond Street look,
                                        before we roonded Hoy.

At Stromness Pier a bonny lass cam strollan roond the deck,
And oh, I wished that I could hae me airms aroond her neck.
Her rosy lips, her curly hair, and her breeks o' corduroy
Were – gone completely frae me mind
                                    before we roonded Hoy.

That morning on the Stromness Pier I gazed into the drink,
And silently I made a prayer the mail boat wadno sink
Or founder in the Pentland Firth wi' me jist but a boy –
But, feth, I start' tae pray shae wad before we roonded Hoy!

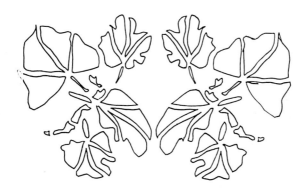

AUTUMN IN ORKNEY

EDDIE BALFOUR

(Eddie Balfour of Rendall is recognised as the finest ornithologist Orkney has produced. He was the RSPB's first full-time officer in Orkney, from 1955 until his death in 1974. He was acknowledged as the world authority on the hen harrier, and he was one of the founders of Orkney Field Club. This account of a group outing to the hills of Hoy appeared in The Scotsman's 'Nature Notes' in 1961.)

Susceptibility to gales, which sweep leaves off our few trees before they have time to colour, accentuates the shortness of autumn here in Orkney. When the equinox is by, winter is on the door-step.

It was, therefore, something of a gamble to hire a boat as late as October 1 for a day among the Hoy Hills, yet it proved to be one of the most cheerful of this wet and sullen season.

A dreamy, pinkish haze intensified the sun's rays, while the breeze invigorated rather than chilled. And freedom from midges and clegs on an island noted for them was not the least blessing. Gannets, immature and adult, dived as we crossed Hoy Sound; Graemsay's wet and flattened sheaves were being restooked. On Hoy we made for the deserted and overgrown manse garden, where a spotted flycatcher disappeared among plum suckers and blackbirds scolded indignantly.

Up by the old Rackwick road, between the hills, the Sandy Loch held an extra foot of floodwater. The poor old road is now little more than a deep and tortuous course for sudden spates, and a jack snipe darted out of it from almost under our feet. Farther on we were delighted to see male and female stonechats, a species which became extinct here during the hard winter of 1940 and is now winning back.

The burn proper appeared to be a westerly redirecting route for migrants: greenfinch, siskin and chaffinch.

With continued depopulation, hill-grazing has almost ceased, rowans and wild rose, birch, willow and juniper are regenerating freely, the two former being richly berried.

One of us climbed to the tops, where red leaves of black bearberry carpeted the ground, still spangled here and there with jet-like berries. This rather local plant seems to favour the 2000-ft contour in Scotland, but, with other alpines, descends below 500 feet in Orkney.

From Grut Fea the rest of the party could be seen, lying prone and gazing intently towards Segal, where a long-eared owl had vanished, apparently appearing reincarnate in the form of an extremely secretive female blackcap.

A mountain hare stood on its hind legs to survey these goings-on, disproving the theory held in some books that the species does not occur in Orkney.

Buzzards have not nested in Orkney recently, but two, perhaps a pair, had been seen several times during the summer, just about here, and now a nest, which might have been theirs, was found.

At any rate, the peregrines were still around and protested strongly at the invasion, and a hen-harrier, kestrel and short-eared owl completed the birds of prey.

Totting up the list of birds seen, in the warm afternoon sunshine, we were surprised to find it came to 50, in a rather restricted area for that time of year.

One last glance at the long Atlantic rollers breaking on white sand, and someone said, 'It will be the last time I'll see Rackwick this year.' With the swift-running tide the boat was soon crossing the sunset path among the diving gannets and within half an hour tied up in Stromness harbour.

We looked across fondly at the Hoy hills, our only Orkney 'mountains,' and saw they had donned a pair of fleecy nightcaps: it was not quite lighting-up time.

'Nature Notes', *The Scotsman*, October 14th 1961.

RACKWICK BAY

HAZEL PARKINS

(On the surface, Orcadians are cheerfully unromantic, in a society whose balance is helped by a built-in block against public expression of emotion. We make up for this in our enjoyment of songs, and particularly country music and traditional music. Hazel Parkins, who wrote this song, has been writing poems since the days when she was a pupil at Stromness Academy. She lives in Kirkwall, and this song, recorded by Billy Jolly to Ronnie Aim's tune 'St Mary's Waltz,' deservedly won Radio Orkney's Song Contest in the early 1980's.)

I think again of summers, when I was just a boy,
Childhood spent in Orkney, by the hills of Hoy,
I'll be home again one day, this time I plan to stay
By the silver sands of Rackwick Bay.

There's a croft high on a hill, in my mind I see it still,
The peatfire burning bright to warm the winter chill,
There's the burn that ripples through, where the wild blue
*   lupins grew;*
I remember Rackwick Bay and you.

I will take the road again by the ancient Dwarfie Stane,
See the valley in the shadows till the sun comes up again,
Hear the lapwings on the moor at the closing of the day,
I'll come back again to Rackwick Bay.

From Australia's golden shore, I hear the wild waves roar,
Creel boats pitch and toss, spray flies like candy floss,
I feel the heather 'neath my feet, hear the great Atlantic beat
On the pebbled beach at Rackwick Bay.

I can't hold back the tears, the passing of the years,
I close my eyes but always the picture still appears,
I'll be home before too long, I'll be home again to stay,
By the silver sands of Rackwick Bay.

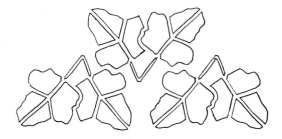

PICTURES FROM THE WIND

DAVID HUTCHISON

(Rackwick is the home of several different people, scattered over the valley. One of the best-known, up the hillside towards the Old Man of Hoy, is Sir Peter Maxwell Davies. Further back down the hill is the abode of David Hutchison, who must be one of the freest and happiest men in Orkney. Far away from the cares of the Orkney mainland, he lives in his little house, enjoying the pleasures of cooking, going for walks with his dogs, yarning with visitors, and writing suitably pointed letters to the local media about the issues of the day. He can also write in reflective mood, as you can see here.)

Orcadians are no different from anyone else in that we all make use of, and marvel at, modern technology. But if mankind has one glaring fault, it is that we are constantly inventing things, then discarding them – then years later, re-inventing them.

In today's modern world, the need for more and more energy has turned our thoughts towards the natural elements, such as wave or wind power. Yet 70 years ago, 12-volt wind generators were a common sight on many an Orkney croft. They were used to provide light and charge lead–acid batteries used for that new novelty, the Wireless. As a child, I can well remember cycling down to the village with a 2-volt accumulator to the garage with a request that it be ready for Saturday so Grandad could listen to Scottish dance music on the radio. With the coming of diesel generators and eventually, mains electricity for the whole of Orkney, these remarkable little machines disappeared – or so I thought.

In 1982 when I came to live in Rackwick, the one thing I missed was TV – such delights as Coronation Street or films and drama which British TV excels in. A small 12-volt TV and a car battery provided strictly limited viewing until the picture shrunk to postage-stamp size. Then the battery was taken down the road to be recharged at a neighbour's house.

However, the problem of battery-charging was solved by Jimmy Moar the local postman who provided a fearsome looking power-plant. A petrol engine 'cannibalised' from an ancient lawn-mower powered a 12-volt dynamo from an old car. And for a time, this 'Heath Robinson' generator functioned perfectly, apart from noise, and the smell of exhaust fumes which filled the house on frosty winter nights.

Then one day, on a shopping trip to Lyness and a chance meeting with a local in a pub, I was asked; 'Know anyone who wants to buy a diesel generator cheap?' Hoy had recently been connected to mains electricity and everyone was disposing of power-plants. And so, I reasoned, here was an opportunity to have mains electricity 'home-made' not only for myself but the two holiday homes next door, and after due consultation with my neighbours, it was agreed to go ahead.

And so, two days later, I arrived back at Moaness Pier on the *Scapa Ranger* with drums of cable, light-bulbs, switches, junction-boxes etc. A week of furious work, cable-laying and electrical plumbing, followed; and we were ready.

It was only when negotiations for the generator began that I got the first shock. For months, Hoy had been swamped with generators for sale. 100 to 150 pounds had been the asking price, but the model I was interested in was a mere £900! No way.

What a dilemma: three houses wired for electricity and not a machine at a price I could afford. Even the local garage man, who weeks earlier had three for sale, was of no help. Then a chance remark changed everything. 'Oh well,' I said, as I turned to leave, 'what a pity I don't have an old Lucas Freelight – then I would be laughing.'

'Hold on,' he said, 'I bought one of them from a farm sale recently. It's here somewhere.' After rummaging through several sheds and outbuildings, we found a head bracket, a tail assembly, two dynamos, a control board, and two wooden blades – and for a mere £30 we had solved our energy needs.

A large wooden pole was erected at the gable end of the stable, and the machine fitted and wired up to the control board and batteries. Then we were 'infuriated' by two days of flat calm. On the third day, a strong breeze sprang up from the west at mid-day, but the blade refused to turn, despite several hand-swings to start it. Then we saw the words on the blade and realised it was on the wrong way.

Once the blade was reversed, the machine roared into life – not before delivering an almighty wallop to the top of my head. I descended from the roof in a cloud of stars, cursing, and arrived in the shed to see the lights come on and the volt-meter register a healthy 10 amps.

That afternoon, I sat nursing a duck-egg-size lump on my head and watching horse racing from Doncaster on TV – courtesy of the wind.

October 1995

THE ISLAND CLIMATE

REV. GEORGE LOW

(Rev. George Low, parish minister in Birsay from 1774 to 1795, pioneered the study of Orkney's natural history, wildlife and archaeology, but suffered much in his lifetime. His work was unpublished and made use of by others, his wife died young, and his eyesight failed. But at last, 200 years on, and through the diligence of Dr Olaf Cuthbert, George Low's writings are being brought into print.)

We seldom have much, if any snow until Christmas, and even then of no long continuance in ordinary years, perhaps a fortnight at a time, tho' there have been instances especially in winter 1771-2 of their continuing much longer. But tho' we seldom have long snows, our seasons are not much more comfortable on that account, for we are frequently amply repaid with rain which is even less agreeable than snow, and as it most commonly falls in great quantities in the winter and harvest seasons, does incredible damage by wasting our corn in harvest and thus rendering our crops very precarious.

Tempestuous winds too are very frequent and hurtful, both in Spring and harvest. These are sometimes so violent as to involve every fruit of the earth in one common destruction. Of this we had a most melancholy instance as late as 1765, when by a westerly storm, the sea was so raised that by the spray of it every vegetable was destroyed, the whole crop suffered, and the whole hopes of the year were blasted, the saltness was perceived on garden plants at the distance of five miles or more within land, the standing corn being caught in the bloom, and were for that year rendered quite useless, a single day defeated the labours of a whole season. Tho' these tempests are happily seldom so universally destructive or make such a general havoc, yet few years pass without their being felt in some measure, and what makes the calamity the more terrible is that it is wholly inevitable.

Thunder is frequent, especially in winter, and some times has a great effect. I have heard of its tearing up the earth, killing animals, and demolishing houses, several instances of which are recorded, and many remembered as the burning of the Steeple in Kirkwall in 1670, and several others which have happened within these late years. These thunder storms are commonly accompanied with heavy rains or hail and these sometimes very sudden, and severe.

We are frequently startled with the appearance of Meteors of several kinds, such as those the Country people call starshots, which every night (according to the weather) are seen sparkling thro' the sky, and other of a more fiery and sulphureous nature, which appear much larger and like balls of fire, whirling large tails after them, these frequently dart thro' the gloom even when the sky to appearance is most serene.

These are frequent, but as yet we are not so much familiarized to them, as to those the Philosophers call the Aurora Borealis or northern lights, and by our country sages on account of the motion Merry Dancers, which are the constant attendants of our clearer evenings, and much relieve the gloom of our long winter nights. They commonly appear at twilight near the horizon of a dun colour, approaching to yellow, sometimes continuing in this state for several hours, without any sensible motion, after which they begin to break out into streams of stronger light, spreading into vast columns and altering slowly into ten thousand different shapes, their colours from all the different tints of yellow to the obscurest russet.

In particular nights we may observe them putting on the appearance of vast columns, having one side very dense and yellow, and the other gradually fainter till they can no longer be distinguished from the rest of the sky.

AURORA

GEORGE MACKAY BROWN

(You could fill an anthology on its own with the work of George Mackay Brown, internationally renowned for his poetry, novels and short stories. He was educated at Stromness Academy, Newbattle Abbey College under Edwin Muir, and Edinburgh University. The town of Stromness, with its tradition of colourful characters and sea travellers, has provided much material for him to draw on, but he has the ability to go far beyond the here and now to explore territory that only the very greatest poets can reach — as in this poem.)

The Arctic girl is out tonight.
(Come to the doors.)
She dances
In a coat of yellow and green patches.
She bends
Over the gate of the stars.

What is she, a tinker lass?
Does she carry flashing cans
From the quarry fires?

I think
She's a princess in a silk gown
She holds (turning)
A bowl of green cut crystal.

Come to the doors!
She is walking about in the north, the winter witch.

From Seal Island Anthology, 1875 in Voyages (1983)

THE WEST IN WIND AND SUN

BESSIE SKEA

(Bessie Skea writes about the Orkney landscape with a keen eye and lyrical style, delicately painting scenes that linger. The colour of a flower half-hidden in cliff-top grass, the curl of water on the tide's edge – each detail is captured perfectly. She comes from Shapinsay, and her husband, Jim Grieve, built the house in Harray where she stays today, continuing each week through her 'Countrywoman' column in The Orcadian to portray a microcosm of Orkney's land, sea and sky. The following was originally written sometime in the 1960's.)

Swans were arched and sailing along the Stenness Loch edge, and fishers encamped on the Harray shore as we drove west. Many ducks and coots dabbled in the valley pools along the Yesnaby road, and clean pigs trotted on free range, one ambling in front of the car.

A brightness hung in the air but the wind blew bitterly, and blue-white heaps of sea moved below the craigs. In the windy, close-grown turf gleamed the primula scotica; we searched each patch of purple for its vivid colour, more royal than the tints of thyme and self-heal appearing stemless in carpet-pile grass. One proud cluster stood match-tall, blowing in the sea-breeze, and this our friend recorded on his colour-film, while my man acted as a windbreak; but still the little stem bent and wavered in eddying gusts, and another was eventually found with a briefer stem, which stood still to be photographed. Trefoil made a perfect contrast, and a miniature bush of eyebright added variety.

Fewer folk were abroad than usual, the west craigs being at least a coat colder than inland. The herons were too far away to visit on an arctic day, but we made plans for another occasion.

Said someone on that drenching Saturday of Shopping Week, while we sought shelter from the rain: 'Surely your man has a lot o' days off afore you can go aboot so much?'

Such a misapprehension I must immediately correct; this man of mine has no day off except Sunday, and the Hoy week-end was his first holiday in three years. On week-day roamings I am either solitary or accompanied by companions with similar interests. My latest outing took me along the west craigs from Yesnaby to Stromness, just three days after our chilly Sunday trip, on a sultry day fleeced with cloud of silver-white, while thunder-heads of inky black rolled and changed to the eastward but did not break. This was a sudden resurgence of summer, in colours intense as technicolor; Mediterranean blue sea, and sky borrowed from remembered years. Primulas gemmed the turf in places where I had not previously seen them; and somewhere along that enchanted coast we found an orchid of unobtrusive but rare beauty, to be admired and photographed. It rose compactly out of broad-based, ground-level, short and tapered leaves; its florets were distinctly hooded above a strap-shaped tongue, and a purple-yellow tone. In the large view-finder it was a lovely thing. Later, consulting all the botanical books we had left behind, we concluded that it could only be a frog orchid, although the flower-spike was shorter and denser than the only illustration I could find; but this could have been the result of environment.

The headlands in front shaded out from brown and green into dark blue, culminating in the clear blue of Hoy with the Old Man standing boldly; along the horizon reached the nebulous shape of the Scottish coastline, and far to the west lay a golden streak between sea and sky. Several fishing-boats were out; the sea was still, except for a slow slight swell sighing against the craigs, occasionally breaking hollowly into caves. Of the three rock stacks, those of North Gaulton are more spectacular than the better-known Castle of Yesnaby. One of these rises erect from a narrowed base in the centre of a geo, and nearby, at a respectful distance from the edge of the shore, we rested to picnic on sandwiches and Ferguzade from a plastic bottle. During our walk this container had changed its shape, now having its sides swollen like a horse with colic; an air-space occupied the top, due to the effervescence in the drink. It was refreshing and sweet, but I was sleepy; the sun beat down, and when I closed my eyes I could see the brilliant orange negative image of the sea. 'I'll get sun-stroke,' I declared, 'an' after the coldest summer on record, that would go down in history!'

Mackerel trails were in the sea, and along this stretch of oily calm I saw momentary black streaks rise and go down again; either the glistening dark bodies of the fish themselves, or something preying upon them. Far out a fishing-boat was gutting fish, for a snow-shower of gulls had descended on his wake. We had missed the heronry, having gone past before recognising Lyra Geo, but two herons flapped great wings with deceptive slowness across a geo farther on. Along Mousland a sheep stared at us and moved out of our way. Here we found a devourer devoured: the body of a black-back which had been partially eaten.

Two burns came out of the hills, burns with dark pebble beds where some have found the glint of gold, for a vein of yellow metal runs somewhere through that brooding land. Out here, I often think, there is room for an entire small community, and here, if I ever write that authentic Orkney tale as I have threatened to do, I will set my scene.

'That's the Black Craig,' we said, as the half-sea-fallen hill rose before us, with its look-out post facing the Atlantic. Underfoot was turf less springy than the close-cushioned thrift we had trod before; here rose a perfect wheel of marguerites, fern-foliage-spoked into the centre, every flower immaculate.

'Grass of Parnassus? No!' We stopped to examine a plant. 'I think we've got something!' I said. The flower standing sturdily at our feet had a square, substantial, ridged stem, typically veined petals but with sepals longer than the petals, and the wrong leaf; this clasped the stem firmly with a very broad base and was twice as long as the normal one. But more Grass of Parnassus grew nearby, and we were forced to conclude that our plant was a freak. Nevertheless, it asked to be photographed.

Through thistled grass we walked uphill, finding a track leading eventually to the Stromness road. But while the clifftops had not wearied us, we found the road hard going under the merciless sun; turning my reversible jacket white-side out relieved me only slightly, and we were glad of a lift for the last long half-mile.

'My, you've got the sun,' they said.

Later that evening came a phone call. 'Are you coman oot tae the cuithes?'

I roused my sleeper out of the chair where he was relaxing, and we got ready for the sea, only to find no car. I snatched up the phone again, but our fishers had left for the shore.

'We'll tak the van,' I suggested.

'Oh no, we won't,' he said firmly.

We called our elder son a few names not usually cast in his direction, for the car could be anywhere in the West Mainland and we were holding up the fishing on an ideal evening.

'I ken whar he is!' I exclaimed suddenly. 'On the loch!'

'Yes, an' I can see him fae here – awey at the opposite side o' the water!'

Our car was three miles away; we made another phone call. 'Please see if you can find that boy an' send him home immediately!' But one cannot communicate with a boat in the middle of a loch, and our son found a large grocery van in place of the car on his eventual return to shore.

We had lost half an hour and the sun had set. All the pools were smoking after the day's heat, and white curls of mist streamed over low fields. A bank of solid blue cloud, with rising pillars, reached out above rose pink. The Bay of Skaill shone glass-green, the loch held the house mirrored on pink and blue, tern wings beat doubled in air and water. Dragon cattle breathed smoke in two spreading plumes. A flat white sea reached out to America.

The black memorial rose on Marwick Head; the horizon lay in sunset colours as we drove down to the shore. The men hauled the boat into a low tide, and we rowed out upon a wide purple sea.

Swells were long and slow; I saw them come, but the motion was scarcely perceptible. I have a fear of small boats because of the nearness of the water; also, this one had a list towards the side my man occupied.

'You couldno' get a better night,' they assured me, and beyond Marwick Head our companion boat moved smoothly into the sunset; we could see a figure hauling fish, and presently the wand I was awkwardly holding moved in my hand. I had to wait for my man to remove the cuithe from the hook; around our feet flapped sleek cold bodies drowning in air.

The water held passing circlets of gold; the craigs were awesome above us, cave-cut and overhanging. Roosting seabirds on their lime-washed rocks called like hens disturbed at bedtime; the sea sounded in blue-floored caves. To the east rose a great round light; it was Jupiter, but seeming so huge that I thought it to be some unchancy thing sent up from earth. Far to the west passed little lights on the horizon, as the fishing-boats we had watched that afternoon went down with their catch to Scrabster.

'You gettan many?' our two row-boats spoke each other as we rounded Marwick Head. The top of the memorial rose like a castle turret; north of us blinked the Brough Lighthouse.

'No; we'd better go home.' We turned down-tide and the sea followed us back to the Noust. Jupiter had climbed high, a great gold lantern over Howe. Getting me ashore proved more difficult than anticipated and I almost took two unwary brothers-in-law overboard into cold black sea, while my man laughed.

We ate fried cuithes at midnight, and dawn was reaching up the sky as we drove home. Through the Marwick valley and along the Twatt road lay a lake of white vapour, and above the hill rose a strange cloud-mirage of buildings in a deep-blue land; and after that wonderful day I was prepared to accept it as such, an image of Norway brought over by the dawn. All the next day I experienced a mild heaving sensation, as if my being still moved gently upon a swelling sunset sea.

Island Journeys (1993)

LIVING BY THE SEA

ELAINE R. BULLARD

(Elaine Bullard has a knowledge about Orkney's vegetation which is unrivalled, and which as the years go by is becoming ever more appreciated by a new generation of admirers. She came to Orkney originally to work in the Claymore Creamery's laboratory, and under a conversational exterior lies a razor-sharp scientific mind that is continually piecing together and revising the picture of the evolution of Orkney's plantlife from the end of the Ice Age to the present day. As well as a hawk-like eye for plant identification, she enjoys – as here – describing the landscape she has worked amongst so closely.)

Many of Orkney's best bird cliffs face the Atlantic and on a wild day the great rollers come pounding in, sending spume and spray and small stones far inland across the wind-browned turf. It seems incredible that the tiny *Primula scotica*, found only in Sutherland, Caithness and Orkney, should like best these exposed places. In June the first flush of flowers will be nearly over, but a few can be found perched cheekily over minute rosettes of mealy leaves. The bird cliffs are a thrilling sight with rank upon rank of guillemots and kittiwakes, and scattered groups of razorbills and shags. On the more broken cliffs, fulmars sit on their solitary eggs or glide backwards and forwards on almost motionless wings. Where there is soft ground near the cliff top, puffins will have burrowed and will fly up, quickly fluttering wings which seem too small, to snatch a clownish look at the intruder.

To the sound of the sea and the sea-birds may be added one of the most stirring of all northern bird calls, from a colony of Arctic skuas nesting on the brown moorland near the sea. It seems right that in these islands where trees are so scarce,

Britain's most northerly heronry should be also on the steep cliffs of a big sea geo, and one year a brood of peregrine falcons – a few pairs still survive in Orkney – were reared in the deserted nest of a pair of herons.

The best place of all to spend a calm June night is on the sea. About the end of the month is the time to visit the cormorant colonies on some of the holms and skerries between the larger islands. As the boat approaches, hundreds of seals, both grey and common, plunge off the rocks. Soon many sleek, inquisitive heads bob up, only to disappear again with sounds for all the world like snorts of disgust. The adult cormorants leave their nests in long low skeins. Their young cry plaintively while the ringing proceeds with speed and efficiency; they are surprisingly soft and warm to handle. We leave as quickly as possible so that they can be brooded again. The boat glides home over water like silk; it is very late but as Eynhallow Sound opens to the north-west the 'holy island' is outlined against the last rays of the setting sun which will rise again quite soon, only a short distance to the north-east.

'Where I Live', *Wild Life Observer*, June 1965

EYNHALLOW

JOHN MOONEY

(John Mooney, 1862-1950, was one of a great generation of Orkney scholars who flourished in the first decades of this century. He was, with Hugh Marwick, Archdeacon Craven, and J. Storer Clouston, a co-founder of the Orkney Antiquarian Society in 1922. He wrote books on St Magnus and on Kirkwall, and one on Eynhallow. In daily life, he was office manager of the firm of Garden's in Kirkwall, but in his books he went deep into Orkney's past.)

Eynhallow lies in the western entrance of the channel or sound which runs south-east between Rousay and the Orkney Mainland, and is about equally distant from those two islands. Viewed from Rousay or Evie on dull, sombre days it appears deserted and uninviting, but the desolate aspect is somewhat relieved by the white surges rising against the dark cliffs or breaking in foam over shelving rocks, as well as by the ebb tide rushing seawards through Burgar and Cutlar Rösts to meet the Atlantic waves. But peaceful and beautiful lies Eynhallow on a day of sunshine – a 'summer isle of Eden' – when only a few fleecy clouds float in the clear, blue sky above it, and the sunbeams play on the darker blue of the encircling currents. Then the green mantle of the isle assumes a brighter tint. How pleasant at such a time to sail in an Orkney 'yawl' from the white sandy beach of Evie, here avoiding the swirling eddies, there taking advantage of the current, and skirting the dangerous skerry where the deep-coloured 'red-ware' twists serpent-like on the surface. As the boat nears the south side of Eynhallow, the sea-weed on the sunken rocks and the sand, at a depth of a few fathoms, presents a variety and richness of colouring surpassing anything to be seen on the Orkney land.

The landing-place is alongside the face of a long, narrow ridge of rock. To the right and left of the rock are nice beaches, fringed at the upper part with pebbles of varying tints of blue and grey; and below that border, silver strand sloping to the sea, and out into the crystal waters. Up on the green sward sheep are pasturing; rabbits, scared by the human intruders, bound off in all directions. If it happens to be the nesting season, the eider duck sitting on her nest at your feet, has less dread, and many of them remain long enough for the camera to be used. Going up an incline for a little distance, you are soon in a position to obtain a view of the lower and southern side of the island. To the right, and on past the Point of Grory, are numbers of pens or folds – locally termed 'crûs' – built mostly of stones from the beach. These enclosures were no doubt used, when the island was inhabited, as shelters for sheep and perhaps cattle; but it is possible that centuries earlier, the monks, skilled in horticulture, had their vegetable gardens in that suitable locality.

A narrow ravine stretches northwards to Ramna-geo, dividing the island into two unequal parts – that to the east being less than a third of the whole area. In some parts of both sides of this 'gap' rocks protrude from the turf. The bottom of it is of a marshy nature, with some grass and many weeds. The ground southward from its entrance was known as the Grange. In some maps the letters of this word are placed so that they run into the ravine, giving the impression that the latter was the Grange. The name Grange on an island with a monastery is significant, and it is necessary that the exact location should be known. The southern portion of Eynhallow is flat, with a rich soil, which continues up the slope to the monastery, and along the western side until the higher land is reached. At the corner of the island which projects farthest into the sound, terminating in Sheep Skerry, is a small 'chin' (or lochan) which becomes dry in summer, and near this are a cluster of modern 'pens' and a sheep house, or store-house.

The Monastery ruins are on rising ground with a southern exposure, and about 150 yards due north of the beach at the

Grand. To the north-east, 75 yards distant from the monastery group, are the remains of the Lower Barns; and at the same distance from the latter, also to the north-east, are Upper Barns. With the exception of the church, with its higher walls and gables, these three clusters of ruins have the appearance, not of ancient and interesting buildings, but of ordinary deserted farm steadings. Once over the stone wall surrounding the monastic buildings, you realise that here is one of Orkney's ecclesiastical treasures – unique relics, in a wonderful state of preservation.

On all sides, except the north, there are traces of various fields, some of which had been enclosed by stone or turf dykes. The remains of a hill-dyke can also be seen, crossing the island. Beyond this, on the northern section, is waste land, most of which is covered with short heather and grasses common to poor, hilly ground, and useful as pasture to a small degree; but nearer the cliffs the soil is bare and devoid of vegetation, owing to the showers of spray in stormy weather. The highest part of the island is little over 100 feet above the assumed mean level of the sea. Here is the usual cairn of stones – the Wart – which usually marks the highest point in all the isles. A thin coating of peat is visible on a restricted portion of the upland. Depressions in the soil indicate that some of it has been 'tirved' for fuel or other purposes.

The Holy Isle faces defiantly the wild Atlantic, its perpendicular cliffs resisting the billows and surges that threaten to overwhelm its sacred soil and buildings. Eastwards from Bowcheek stretch bold rugged rocks with narrow chasms; and nearer Ramnageo, as the tide recedes, flat ledges of smooth rock, resembling the broad pavement of a street, seem to rise suddenly from the ocean depth, like the isle itself, in the days when it was believed to vanish for a time from mortal view, and once more to reappear in its wonted place. Ramnageo (the Orkney form of the Old Norse *Hrafnagjá* – Raven's Gap) is the most picturesque spot in Eynhallow. It penetrates deep into the rocks, the sea being held back at high water by a beach of pebbles and large round stones. The hollow, or ravine, already mentioned is really a continuation of Ramnageo, and had it been deeper, what is now one isle would have been two smaller islets. South-west of the Geo rises a steep brae which culminates at the Wart. In the face of this brae is the well, Keldamurra, which is one of the land-marks used by the fishermen of Rousay and Evie when returning from the fishing grounds north of Eynhallow. Dangerous rocks border the passage into Ramnageo, and on the east side are fine specimens of broad flat rocks, and above these brown and grey cliffs, highest at the landward end of the Geo, and forming the headland, Fint. An artist could find here subjects worthy of his highest skill.

Dietrichson declared the surroundings of Eynhallow to be 'scenery of enchanting beauty, just such as the mediæval monks were accustomed to choose for the sites of their monasteries.' There is, indeed, beauty of surroundings, but these are also romantic. At the Wart, on a bright day, the panorama is one worth going to the isle to see. On the Mainland towards Birsay the gigantic cliffs of Costa Head look across the sound to Scabra Head, Rousay – the other sentinel that stands guard over the little green isle with 'a roaring röst on every side.' The purple of the terraced hills, mellowed by the sunshine, forms a charming background to the deep green of the cultivated fields stretching along the shore. The rocks and headland nearer the Atlantic recall the daring attack of Sweyn Asleifson and his men when they caught Earl Paul and carried him captive to distant Atholl.

Close by, in Rousay, is the land of the old Udal property of Brough, held by Craigies and Halcros, who were also heritors of Eynhallow. In a picturesque situation, unequalled elsewhere in the island, stands the mansion house of Westness. The great Udaller, Sigurd, steadfast friend and 'hirdman' of Earl Paul, lived and held sway at Westness 800 years ago. To the south, on the other side of Eynhallow Sound, the fertile fields of Evie skirt the shore and slope upwards to the moss and heather of the hills which separate that parish from Birsay. Down the sound, where 'with eddy and whirl the sea-tides curl,' Aikerness is seen with its beautiful sands and links. When Norsemen were no longer Chiefs of the Isles, the influential

Scottish Ballendens (or Bellendens) of Stenness, superiors of Eynhallow, had their principal residence at Aikerness. A few miles beyond, part of Wyre, like a long green ness, is seen reaching out towards Gairsay and its big round hill. Imagination calls up pictures of Norse galleys with striped sails gliding past those isles on their way to the Orkney Parliament and Court of Law at Tingwall.

Eynhallow: The Holy Island of the Orkneys (1923)

THE STORM

ERIC LINKLATER

(In Eric Linklater's later years, and after his death in 1974, critical fashion turned away from him cruelly. His unfashionability may in part have been, unfairly, a reaction to his earlier public popularity. Today, we can look more objectively at him and recognise that he was popular and successful simply because he was so very, very good. The sweep of history that flows through his books, the influence of fate, the grim humour of survival, are all qualities that should prepare the ground for a present-day rediscovery. The following passage from The Men of Ness shows his mastery of language, in description of surroundings and control of narrative. It is not surprising to note that his father was a sea-captain and his grandfather a whaling harpooner.)

The wind was in the north-east. There was calm water in the sound between Eynhallow and Rousay, but when they came from under the lee of Rousay there was a lively sea running. The Skarf lay somewhat astern of the Skua.

All the men were in good spirits and spoke cheerfully about the voyage. With such a wind they would soon cross the Pictland Firth and come to the west side of Scotland. Because of the rising sea Skallagrim bade them take in their shields, that hang outside on the gunwales, and stow them away.

They sailed westwards along the north coast of the Mainland of Orkney, from Costa Head to the Broch of Birsay, and came speedily to the Broch with the wind on their starboard quarter. When they had passed it they altered course to the south-west, and the wind was squarely behind them.

Skallagrim had his crew busy shifting some ballast, for the Skua was rather by the head. The men worked with a will. They were all good men, very sturdy and warlike, and most of them well used to ships. A few of them were young, and this was their first viking cruise, but some were oldish men who had sailed in many seas, far east in the Baltic and south by Spain, harrying there under famous captains. Some had fought in King Harald's wars, and two had sailed with Biorn Ironside, Ragnar Hairybreeks's son.

The Skua was sailing faster than the Skarf, and Erling's ship fell more astern. Skallagrim bade his men take a reef in the sail, that they might not part company.

Now they were farther from the land, and on the larboard side they could see all the west coast of Orkney. It stood like a wall with breaches here and there where the sea had broken down the cliffs and made small bays and geos. It was a bad coast to be wrecked on. It had a friendless look to all except the sea-birds, and they nested on the cliffs in great numbers. There were gulls of all kinds, skarfs and puffins, and eider-ducks, and trimly flying kittiwakes. In some places the cliffs were white with their droppings.

Erling's ship came up and sailed abreast of the Skua. The men shouted to each other across the sea between them, and waved their caps.

It grew more difficult to steer, for the wind was rising and did not blow steadily now, but came in hard gusts and then fell for a little while to a light breeze. The gusts became stronger all the time, and then the ships leapt forward with foam curling before them and hissing along their sides. The masts creaked, the stays stretched taut, and the sails stood out hard and round. And the wind was backing into the north.

There came a long fierce gust, and afterwards for some time a light and pleasant breeze. The sun shone brightly and the farther sea was blue with thin white crests on it. Then another squall came, darkening the sea and flattening the waves. It came swiftly, spreading like a fan, and struck hard on the ships. And now the wind came out of the north.

Kol said, 'It seems that Thorlief was right when he said it was a backing wind.'

But Skallagrim said, 'We shall be over the Firth before it can back far, and there is plenty of shelter on the other side.'

The day became darker and the sun was covered. To the west a brown mass of clouds appeared, growing larger and reaching into the sky. And now when the wind slackened there was the faint far-off noise of a greater wind. But Skallagrim held to his course and Erling sailed a little distance away, on the weather side of him.

Kol said, 'I think it were best if we turned and ran in towards Hoy and took some shelter under the high land there. For if the wind grows stronger while we are in the open Firth it may go badly with us.'

Skallagrim rubbed his chin at that, but did not answer.

Then two or three of the older men on board came to him and said the same thing, and while they were disputing they saw Erling wave to them from the Skarf and point landwards.

'Have it your own way,' said Skallagrim, and changed his course and stood in towards Hoy.

That is the highest land in Orkney. There are two hills there, black and rugged, and most often there is cloud about their tops. On the west side the cliffs come sheer out of the sea. From the Kame of Hoy to the Sow they are more than a thousand feet high, and straight as a wall. Then they fall lower, and the coast turns in to a bay called Rackwick, and from there runs south-east. There is no landing-place on that side of Hoy except Rackwick, nor can a landing be made at Rackwick when the wind blows strongly from the west.

The ships were well to the west of Hoy and somewhat south of the high cliffs. They could see into Rackwick. Now they sailed for the shelter of Hoy and had the wind on their larboard quarter.

But before they were near land it fell away altogether, and they tossed about in the sea without steering-way. A light squall came and filled the sails. It raced on and left them tossing again. But another came, stronger than the first, and behind it the sea was all dark and the wind came steadily and blew gale-strong. And now the wind had gone farther round and came from the north-west.

It blew so strongly they could do nothing but run before it.

'This is a poor course for Man,' said Kol.

Skallagrim said, 'Now we can find no lee under Hoy. We must run through the Firth and take shelter east of Scotland.'

Kol said, 'There will be ebb-tide in the Firth.'

'Tide or no tide, that is the way we must go,' said Skallagrim.

'Erling will fare worse than us,' said Kol. 'He has less freeboard.'

'Erling must fare as he can,' said Skallagrim, 'for there is nothing else to do.'

The Skarf fell somewhat astern of the Skua again when they ran into the Firth and came against the tide. The ebb runs eastward there and is a strong tide. With the wind against it there was a heavy sea and the Skarf laboured in it. Erling set men to bale. The sea rose wildly and the waves fell in confusion between the wind and the ebb.

Now the gale broke on them in all its strength and roared about them. The Skua drove before it, beating the tide, and plunged in the heavy sea. It was not easy to steer it then. Kol often looked backwards to the Skarf. There was little comfort in Erling's ship, for the steep waves broke about them and they shipped a lot of water. The men there baled steadily.

There are two islands in the Firth called Stroma and Swona. They are small islands, not high, but rocky. At the north end of Stroma and the south end of Swona there are fierce roosts. The roost of Stroma is called the Swelkie, and that of Swona the Tarf. There the tide boils and tumbles in great whirlpools, so that even on a calm day the waves leap up, white-hooded, and in stormy weather no ship can live there. Skallagrim's course lay midway between Swona and Stroma.

The Skua came nearer to the islands, and on the larboard bow the waves of the Tarf rose fiercely and the wind flung the spray from them in a great cloud. But on the starboard bow the Swelkie of Stroma boiled like a giant's cauldron, and it looked as though the sea lifted itself in great ridges and leaped out of huge holes.

The Men of Ness (1932)

A NATURE MISCELLANY

HUGH MARWICK

(Hugh Marwick is justly regarded as one of the greatest scholars Orkney has produced. His works on dialect and place-names gave him an international reputation and produced a number of classic books and papers. He came to university late, having had to work by day to save up money to pay for his course, and study in the evenings, but once there, a brilliant academic career followed, which led to his becoming Rector of Kirkwall Grammar School and then Director of Education for the county. His feelings for Orkney, and particularly for Rousay where he was born, often come through in his writing.)

To judge from place-name evidence several birds must have been characteristic of these isles from of old, and of these the shag or cormorant may well head the list. The local name for either bird is skarf, and names such as Skarvataing or Skarrataing, Skarraklett, or Skarf Skerry are to be found all over Orkney. These birds are rarely if ever seen inland except when in flight, but around the coasts it is no exaggeration to say that individuals, or more usually flocks, are never out of view. Though either shag or cormorant may be termed a skarf the latter was formerly differentiated in some islands by other names. In Westray it was, and probably still is, known as the hiblin, the same word as the Faroese *hiplingur* – that is, 'the hipped-one,' from the whitish patch seen on the under flank of the bird when in flight. In Rousay it was known as the lairblade or lairblading, a name derived from the same white patch, and meaning 'the thigh-patched one,' from Old Norse *lær*, thigh, and *blettr*, a spot or patch. These birds are never used as food in Orkney, but during the recent hungry years many of them, as well as other wild birds, are said to have been shot and sent south for sale, and it is not improbable that in London hotels or elsewhere the reader may have been regaled with roast shag camouflaged as wild duck!

The oyster-catcher is the island emblem of the Faroes, when it goes by the name of *tjaldur*. The Orkney form of that word is chaldro, and the presence of the bird from of old is attested by such names as Chaldro Rock or Cholder Tuack. It is still today one of the commoner birds along our shores, where its conspicuous plumage renders it hardly less noticeable than its piercing call, which makes it the true sentinel of the beach.

The raven is another bird still occasionally to be seen in Orkney, but to judge from the several Ramna Geos or Ramla Geos (raven geos) in the cliffs it was probably more numerous in former times. A geo is a creek or indentation in the coastline, but in the case of a Ramna Geo it is always flanked by high and precipitous crags.

The eider is an all-the-year resident, and Itherie Geo is a name for several creeks which were evidently favourite places of resort (O.N. *æðr*, eider). At one place on the Rousay coast is a rather unusual stretch of smooth pavement-like rocks, sloping gently down to the water's edge, with a number of caves in the cliffs behind. A common word today for a cave in the cliffs, especially a high-roofed cave, is the Scots ha' (hall), and these Rousay caves are known by the resounding name of The Ha's o' Ither Hellyie. It is rather difficult to determine whether the Hellyie refers to the caves (O.N. *hellir*, a cave) or the flat rocks below (O.N. *hella*, a flat rock or stone), but on those rocks eiders love to parade and rest, and have done so apparently for centuries. In Iceland eiders are protected on account of their down, and even today in Orkney anyone who shoots an eider, or dunter, as it is now commonly called, is looked on as a bit of a cad.

One of the most familiar birds to be seen cruising over the sounds and firths is the gannet or solan goose. Its breeding place is an isolated pillar rock known as the Stack, about four miles from Sule Skerry, which is thirty-seven miles due west of Marwick Head in Birsay. The Old Norse name for the bird was *sula*, the word from which Sule Skerry derives its name, and that it has bred there for at least seven hundred years is apparent from the fact that the names *Sulna-sker* for the Skerry and *Sulna-stape* for the Stack are both mentioned in the *Hakon Saga*, which dates from about 1266.

The gannet is rarely if ever seen on land (except, of course, at its nesting grounds), but several years ago the writer was informed of a most curious incident which is also recorded by Buckley and Harvie-Brown in their *Fauna of Orkney*. It is told there as follows:

'In July 1863, while Dr James Logie of Kirkwall was returning from visiting a patient in Harray, he succeeded in capturing a fine specimen of the Solan Goose in the following manner. As he was driving along the Stromness Road by the Bay of Firth he was suddenly startled by the appearance of a huge white bird which kept swooping and dashing about the lantern of his gig. The night was very dark, and as the bird's screams seemed unearthly enough for anything it was some little time before Dr Logie ascertained the precise nature of his visitant. Presently he observed the bird alight in a deep ditch by the roadside, and getting out of his gig, he, with the aid of the lantern, so dazzled the bird that it was easily captured. A closer inspection showed it to be a remarkably fine specimen of the Solan Goose. The bird is now stuffed and in Dr Logie's possession.'

Dr Logie died a few weeks after celebrating his centenary in 1920, but in all the course of that long life he can hardly have had a more unexpected or startling *rencontre*.

In the dedication of his *Stickit Minister* to Robert Louis Stevenson S. R. Crockett wrote that the scene of the book was laid among the moors, 'where about the graves of the martyrs the whaups are crying, *his* heart remembers how.' 'Ay, by God, I do,' wrote Stevenson in acknowledgment, adding that he could never read those words without tears springing to his eyes. To a native of Orkney in a distant land the cry of the whaup (curlew) would be similarly evocative, but many other things would be no less so. Each individual, of course, would have his or her more personal memories, and we can suggest but a few that might be common to all: the cries of lapwings in spring and the chorus of corncrakes on a still summer night; the smell of peat smoke or of that from heather fires as it floats across from isle to isle on a March evening; the rich, almost overpowering scent of meadowsweet or Yule grass along a burn or ditch in summer, or the more delicate and elusive fragrance of 'the banks' along the shore 'where the wild thyme blows,' along with eyebright, Our Lady's bedstraw and all the other familiar little flowers that deck the Orkney turf; wide sweeps of moorland covered as by a ground mist with waving white cottongrass in July, or the purple glow of a hillside in August when the heather-bells are in bloom; not least perhaps the cosy comfortable look of farm-steadings in harvest after the crops have been tidily secured in the stackyards and all is snug for the winter.

These are but a few of the sights and sounds and scents that are characteristic of Orkney, and we have not yet mentioned what is in a sense the most characteristic of all — the ever-changing panoply of sea and sky. Grey, sombre days are many, but there are others when a brisk north wind, as Henryson says, has

> …purifyit the air,
> And sched the misty cloudis fro the sky.

On such days the intense blue of the sky above is reflected in the sea below, so that it can vie with the Mediterranean, and the colouring of the isles is all heightened as if they were new washed. To the hard brilliance of such a scene the coming of sunset brings the greatest possible contrast of soft, mellow, constantly changing tones, while the western sky displays such a riot of colour as is quite indescribable. Orkney has many claims to beauty, but nothing that can surpass the glory of its sunsets, unless it be the pageantry of the Merry Dancers, the Aurora Borealis. Lest the writer may be thought prejudiced it may be permissible to quote the moving words of one unbiased

49

stranger – no other than the German Vice-Admiral von Reuter, who was in command of the surrendered German Fleet in Scapa Flow after the 1914-18 war. In his book *Scapa Flow: The Account of the Greatest Scuttling of All Time*, as translated by Lieut. Commander Mudie, R.N., he wrote as follows:

'The scenery around us was really harsh and desolate. Water, mountains, otherwise nothing. And yet this forgotten corner of the earth had its attractions, its beauty – not by day, during glaring sunlight or when the rainclouds painted everything grey on grey, but in the evening or by night. Then it was that the Northern Lights would cast their rays like searchlights over the clouds and light them to a yellow hue, then again pour themselves over the whole firmament in a single sea of fire. And the sunsets, wonderful in their coloured splendour. It was during a May evening, the sun sank to the horizon at a late hour, and all the colour of which it seemed possessed was poured over the evening sky; the spectacle was overpowering and enchanting. And then, as though this were not of sufficient splendour, the Northern Lights flung their fiery streams into the blaze – the clouds were fired, and in their flaming fire rose the dark naked cliffs of the mountains of Orkney. There is yet a God!'

Orkney (1951)

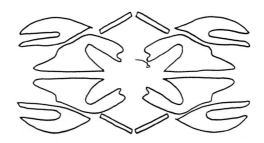

THE GERMAN FLEET IN SCAPA FLOW

CMDR. YORCK VON REUTER

(Admiral von Reuter's connection with Orkney was continued by his eldest son, writing in 1989 on the story of the German Fleet.)

Unser Leben gehet dahin
wie große Schiffe die sinken.

Our life passes away
like great ships as they sink

This inscription was found by accident in the vault of Field Marshal Derfflinger (1609-95), in the small village church where he was finally laid to rest. It was found on the 21st June, 1919, the exact day when the battleship SMS *Derfflinger* went to its grave together with the Imperial German Fleet in Scapa Flow.

This year is the 70th anniversary of that happening – a date to be remembered. Newspapers in Germany and the UK have been recording the anniversary, and I am reminded of it by the battle-flag of SMS *Markgraf* which decorates the wall behind my desk.

What led to this unique event in history, when a whole fleet of 74 warships sank themselves within a matter of hours, an action which echoed around the world? On that day, after four years of world war, the peace treaty was to have been agreed upon.

But it turned out to be a day of perplexity rather than joy to both sides. The Armistice had to be prolonged, and it was only on the 28th June, 1919, that the treaty of Versailles was concluded. By this time the German Fleet did not exist any more – it lay on the bottom of Scapa Flow. This fleet had been considered one of the reasons for entering the war, and was to have been divided up amongst the victorious nations.

Grand-Admiral von Tirpitz had built his fleet at the beginning of the 20th century with the idea of 'the unacceptable risk' in mind, that the German Imperial Navy would be so powerful that attack by sea on the German coasts could only be undertaken at considerable risk. This objective was fulfilled, and during that world war those coasts were never threatened; furthermore, any forcing of the straits into the Baltic and thence to Russia was prevented, however much the Allies may have desired it.

After four years of war against the whole world, the strength of the Kaiser's Reich was broken, and along with it the morale of the German Fleet.

My father, Admiral Ludwig von Reuter, as Commander of the interned fleet, took advantage of the fateful occasion to save the Imperial Fleet from the disgrace of surrender. When the Armistice was terminated on 21st June, 1919, he was not informed of the subsequent decision to prolong it, but was convinced that war conditions were reinstated. He then put an end to the fleet in honour by sinking the ships.

Years later, it was found that valuable treasure was covered by the waters of Scapa Flow, and salvage began, which turned out to be a hard job with many problems. Today, several German ships are still on the bottom of Scapa Flow, along with the Royal Naval ships, *Royal Oak* and *Vanguard*. They rest peacefully together on the bottom; the fighting has ended. May this peaceful resting together of the ships of two nations once at war serve as a symbol of lasting concord.

Was vergangen, kehrt nicht wieder,
Ging es jedoch leuchtend nieder
leuchtets lange noch zurück.

What has passed away does not return.
But if it disappeared in glory
its light shines on for long.

Foreword to The Naval Wrecks of Scapa Flow (1989)

KÖNIG

PETER L. SMITH

(Peter Smith lives in North Wales and has been diving in Scapa Flow for many years. His detailed research captures the spirit of the ships which fought at Jutland, among them the battleship which led the line there and now lies in about 35 metres of water off Cava.)

Seiner Majestät Schiff *König* was the name ship of the fourth class of German Dreadnought battleships, successors to the *Kaiser*-class Dreadnoughts. *König* herself served as Flagship of the Third Squadron of the High Seas Fleet, and under her command were her three sister ships (*Markgraf, Kronprinz Wilhelm* and *Grosser Kurfürst*), and three of the *Kaiser*-class battleships.

The *Kaiser*-class vessels – *Kaiser* herself, *Prinzregent Luitpold, Kaiserin, König Albert* and *Friedrich der Grosse* – were magnificent ships, but the *König*-class battleships were even better. They were built as answer to the first of the British super-Dreadnoughts, which had been the first battleships to carry all their main armament along the ship's centreline, with fore and aft turrets superimposed. This arrangement enabled all the main guns to be fired together on a single broadside.

König had been included in the 1911 Naval Estimates of the Reichstag, and was launched on March 1st, 1913. Following fitting out and commissioning, she joined the High Seas Fleet on August 10th, 1914, six days after the outbreak of war. The cost of building *König* had been 43 million Marks, equivalent to about £2.25 million then.

Contemporary British ships cost about £1.8 million each, and the greater price of the German warships reflects the effort to make them as unsinkable as possible, to withstand a British broadside. The German designers protected the vital parts of each ship with the thickest and densest armourplate it could carry, and the hull was subdivided into as many watertight compartments as possible, to restrict the effects of flooding after holing. A compartment could be deliberately flooded to maintain stability, in the case of damage to a compartment on the opposite side of the ship.

The sheer size of *König* is difficult to take in from figures alone. The ship was 576 feet long – almost the length of two football pitches – and at the widest section of the hull she had a beam of 100 feet. When fully loaded with fuel and ammunition her foredeck was 22 feet above the water, her bridge 30 feet higher, and the spotting top on the foremast above the bridge was 100 feet above water level. The average modern two-storey house stands at about 22 feet to the ridge tiles, so it will be appreciated what an awesome sight *König* must have made. She would have been resplendent in her pale grey livery, teak decks shining white, and black-and-white cross of the Imperial German Ensign flying at her mainmast, and the silver-and-gold crown of the King of Prussia emblazoning the *wappen* on each side of her bow.

König's first action, although the ship fired not a single shot, was in support of the three battlecruisers, *Lützow, von der Tann* and *Moltke,* which arrived off Lowestoft early on the morning of 25th April, 1916, and in the space of ten minutes demolished 200 houses by shelling. The three ships then steamed north and repeated the exercise on Great Yarmouth. A small force of British light cruisers came on the scene and tried to delay them until the Grand Fleet could arrive, but the Germans decided on this occasion to prefer caution and retreated to their bases on the River Jade.

It was almost halfway through the war before the two Fleets met in force at the Battle of Jutland. Admiralty intelligence received reports that the German battlecruisers were about to leave port on another raid, and the British Grand Fleet put to sea on the 30th May, 1916, to carry out a sweep across the northern sector of the North Sea towards the Skagerrak.

The Battle Fleet under the command of Admiral Sir John Jellicoe set out from Scapa Flow with its 24 battleships and three battlecruisers, along with escorting destroyers and scouting cruisers. The plan was for it to rendezvous off the Skagerrak with the Battlecruiser Fleet of Vice-Admiral Sir David Beatty, on his way from Rosyth with six battlecruisers, four fast battleships and attendant destroyers and scouts.

Meanwhile, the German Scouting Group of the High Seas Fleet, with five battlecruisers and their torpedo boat screen and scouting cruisers, had put to sea, and by the afternoon of 31st May, they came into contact with Beatty's ships. The two forces had been steaming on almost parallel courses, out of sight of one another over the horizon, and quite possibly might never have met, but for the chance that a Danish merchant steamer, the *N. J. Fjord*, was on route midway between them. As a neutral ship, she was stopped and given a routine search by the German torpedo boats, *B109* and *B110*, who were out on the edge of the German battlecruiser force. Meanwhile, the British light cruiser, *Galatea*, scouting on the edge of her own fleet, sighted the Danish ship and went over with the same intentions as the Germans. The *Galatea* noticed steam from the departing German torpedo boats, and they themselves saw her coming into sight and signalled their flotilla leader, SMS *Elbing*. By 15.45 in the afternoon, the two groups of battlecruisers had manoeuvred into position against each other, and furious firing commenced. A series of salvoes from *von der Tann* struck the last ship on the British battlecruiser line, HMS *Indefatigable*, which blew up in a massive explosion from her magazines.

The four fast *Queen Elizabeth*-class battleships of Beatty's force (*Barham, Valiant, Warspite* and *Malaya*), forming the Fifth Battle Squadron, had been left some miles astern due to a signalling error, but they now started to catch up with the action, opening fire from nearly eleven miles away with their 15-inch guns. Their arrival on the scene began to redress the balance, but not before another of the six British battlecruisers, HMS *Queen Mary*, had suffered a similar fate to the *Indefatigable* from the 12-inch shells of *Derfflinger*.

By this time, however, the news came through from the cruiser, *Southampton*, scouting some miles ahead of the action, that it was not merely the German battlecruisers who were at sea. The earlier Admiralty monitoring of the German radio signals had misinterpreted one key message, which would have told them that the force of ships putting to sea that day was in fact the full High Seas Fleet. Steaming northwards now at full speed towards the action were the six divisions of the Battle Fleet, comprising 16 Dreadnought battleships and six pre-Dreadnoughts, commanded by Vice-Admiral Scheer in the *Friedrich der Grosse* and led by Rear Admiral Paul Behncke in *König*.

This was the moment for which the British strategists had so long planned and hoped, and Beatty switched tactics to draw the German ships north towards the guns of Jellicoe's battleships, on their way from Scapa Flow. He first took his own ships south, to let the German Battle Fleet catch sight of them, and then swung back north, to run before the Germans using his superior speed. By the time the last ships in his line were altering course to turn northward, they had come into range of *König*'s guns, which inflicted damage on *Malaya* and *Warspite*. *Malaya* took the brunt of this punishment, and many of her crew now lie buried at the Naval Cemetery at Lyness, on Hoy.

The chase north became close. The British ships had been designed to achieve speeds of up to 25 knots, but in practice barely reached 24, while the lead German ships, *König* and her sisters, were reaching speeds of up to 23 knots and maintaining a continuing fire on the British battleships. *Malaya*, despite her own casualties, managed to score some hits on *König*, causing devastation on board but failing to affect the German ship's speed or fighting power. Eventually the British drew out of range of the German guns, and now from this safe distance could continue to shell their pursuers due to the greater range of their larger armament.

The chase lasted little more than an hour, before the Germans found themselves confronted by the massed ships of Jellicoe's Battle Fleet, stretched out across the horizon in front of them to concentrate their fire on the warships entering the trap. *König* sustained further hits, some secondary armament being put out of action, and the Flagship of the German battlecruiser force, *Lützow*, already damaged in the earlier battlecruiser action, was reduced to a hulk and withdrew to sink. By this time Admiral Scheer was pulling back out of the trap, turning his whole Fleet around at once to take his line south and out of reach of the British guns. Due to the vast amount of smoke generated by the ships' boiler fires and the burning cordite from their guns, the Fleets lost sight of each other, but during this brief but furious action, *Derfflinger* found another victim when the smoke and mist lifted for a moment to reveal the luckless battlecruiser, *Invincible*, silhouetted against the northern horizon, less than 10,000 yards from her guns.

In the darkness of the smoke, Scheer turned eastwards to try to escape towards his bases, but found he was again heading towards the centre of Jellicoe's Battle Fleet, which had steamed round to cut him off. Scheer ordered his damaged battlecruisers to attack the British with no regard for the consequences, but again the guns pounded the German ships, and again *König*, still leading the German line, was hit, and this time holed. Confusion and panic broke out amongst the German Fleet, with some ships turning away without waiting for orders, causing others to stop or even go astern to avoid collisions. Admiral Behncke in *König* adroitly saved the situation by turning into the wind and creating a smokescreen to cover the German withdrawal, while German torpedo boats closed in on the British Fleet to attack the battleships, creating another smokescreen to hid their own capital ships. This action worked, with the British battleships having to take evasive measures to avoid the torpedoes, and during this time the German Fleet was lost to sight in the smoke, mist and now failing light.

König was battered but still afloat, and during the night headed for home, carrying 1,600 tons of sea water in flooded compartments, with armour plate stoved in, her foredeck and casement decks blown open, and her bows down in the water. Even when she reached the protective shelter of the German minefields, she was now drawing so much water forward that she had to wait for a high tide to clear a sandbank off the Jade to berth in Wilhelmshaven for repairs.

König's final voyage was to meet up again with the British Fleet to enter internment in Scapa Flow. She was unable to raise steam for the voyage at this time, as due to inactivity and lack of maintenance some condenser tubes were leaking. Following re-tubing, *König* joined her sisters in Scapa Flow on 6th December, 1918.

The Naval Wrecks of Scapa Flow (1989)

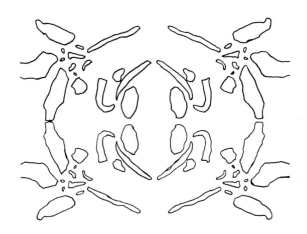

WITH THE LIGHTHOUSE YACHT IN ORKNEY

SIR WALTER SCOTT

(As Sheriff of the sea-bordering county of Selkirk, Sir Walter Scott was a Commissioner of Northern Lights, and so able to join the party for their annual seaborne tour of lighthouse inspection in the autumn of 1814. Scott had just published his first novel, Waverley; the Orkney part of the voyage was to give him the inspiration for his second.)

Wednesday 17th August 1814. Off Stromness. Went on Shore after breakfast and found W. Erskine and Marjoribanks had been in this town all last night, without our hearing of them or they of us. No letters from Abbotsford or Edinburgh. Stromness is a little, dirty, straggling town which cannot be traversed by a cart, or even by a horse, for there are stairs up and down, even in the principal streets. We paraded its whole length like turkeys in a string, I suppose to satisfy ourselves that there was a worse town in the Orkneys than the metropolis, Kirkwall.

We climb, by steep and dirty lanes, an eminence rising above the town and commanding a fine view. An old hag lives in a wretched cabin on this height and subsists by selling winds. Each captain of a merchant-man, between jest and earnest, gives the old woman sixpence and she boils her kettle to procure a favourable gale. She was a miserable figure; upwards of ninety, she told us and dried up like a mummy. A sort of clay-coloured cloak, folded over her head, corresponded in colour to her corpse-like complexion. Fine light-blue eyes and nose and chin that almost met and a ghastly expression of cunning, gave her quite the effect of Hecate. She told us she remembered *Gow the pirate,* who was born near the House of Clestrom and afterwards commenced buccanier. He came to his native country about 1725, with a *snow* which he commanded, carried off two women from one of the islands and committed other enormities. At length, while he was dining in a house in the island of Eda, the islanders headed by Malcolm Laing's grandfather made him a prisoner and sent him to London, where he was hanged. While at Stromness he made love to a Miss Gordon, who pledged her faith to him by shaking hands, an engagement which – in her idea – could not be dissolved without her going to London to seek back again her 'faith and troth' by shaking hands with him again after execution!

We left our pythoness, who assured us there was nothing evil in the intercession she was to make for us, but that we were only to have a fair wind through the benefit of her prayers. She repeated a sort of rigmarole which I suppose she had ready for such occasions and seemed greatly delighted and surprised with the amount of our donation, as everybody gave her a trifle, our faithful Captain Wilson making the regular offering on behalf of the ship.

So much for buying a wind. Bessy Millie's habitation is airy enough for Aeolus himself, but if she is a special favourite with that divinity he has a strange choice. In her house I remarked a quern, or hand-mill. A cairn, a little higher, commands a beautiful view of the bay, with its various entrances and islets. Here we found the vestiges of a bonfire, lighted in memory of the battle of Bannockburn, concerning which every part of Scotland has its peculiar traditions. The Orcadians say that a Norwegian prince, then their ruler, called by them Harold, brought 1,400 men of Orkney to the assistance of Bruce and that the King, at a critical period of the engagement, touched him with his scabbard saying, 'The day is against us.'

'I trust,' returned the Orcadian, 'your grace will *venture again*;' which has given rise to their motto and passed into a proverb.

On board at half-past three and find Bessy Millie a woman of her word, for the expected breeze has sprung up, if it but last us till we double Cape Wrath. Weigh anchor (I hope) to bid farewell to Orkney.

'Northern Lights', included in Lockhart's *Memoirs of the Life of Sir Walter Scott, Bart.* (1837-8)

ALL AT SEA

BRYCE WILSON

(As head of Orkney's Museums Service, Bryce Wilson has been responsible for the development of Tankerness House Museum and the Kirbuster and Corrigall Farm Museums, as well as the continued development of the separately-owned Stromness Museum with its maritime themes. He is a skilled artist, having trained at Gray's School of Art in Aberdeen, and he has a specialist knowledge of Orkney's maritime past and its links with the world's oceans, as when writing here of Stromness's sea-captains.)

In the days when islands regarded the sea as a highway, and an important source of food, Orkneymen were as much at home there as on the land.

In wartime, many were pressed into, or volunteered for, the Navy. For a few, buying a commission could lead to a distinguished naval career. Lieutenant James Miller conducted a successful naval engagement against a French frigate in the Bay of Naples in 1809, while in command of HMS *Cyane*; Lieutenant James Robertson was commander of HMS *Beresford* during an attack on the American squadron at the battle of Plattsburg in 1812.

Young men could escape to adventure on foreign-bound merchantmen, particularly in the 19th century, when the British Empire had a huge merchant fleet, and large crews were needed for 'Cape-Horners.'

While the sailor was romanticised in popular literature, life was seldom comfortable below decks, and often dangerous in the rigging above. There were other hazards: a Stromness man, Tammy Corrigall, went bathing in a southern sea, and lost both forearms to a shark....

Many sea-captains lived in the town; their wives could accompany them on long voyages, and some of their children were born at sea. In 1875, Captain James Skinner wrote from Napier (New Zealand): 'My Dear Wife... I will take you with me next Voyage if spared. This is a very lonely place to be in we lay about 2 miles from the Shore and the time hangs Very long especially when there is no one to Speak to and I never go on shore. There is lots of all kinds of Fish to be caught there is a little amusement in that. And sometimes I have a game of cards with young Kruse....

Mrs Corrigall of Farafield Lane sailed with her husband for fifteen years, 'Over a great part of the Pacific... and away north to Vladivostok, in Siberia, before there were proper charts for that region. Japan, China... India, South Africa, Australia, New Zealand, North and South America; up the Mediterranean and the Baltic....'

Sea Haven (1992)

GROWING UP WITH THE SEA

CAPT. ROBERT L. SUTHERLAND

(Through the Stromness Sea School, which he was in charge of for many years, Robbie Sutherland has shaped a whole generation of Orcadians, giving them the skills and attitudes and example to command oceangoing vessels, oil support ships, and a fleet of modern fishing vessels. Before going into teaching, he spent many years in the Merchant Navy, including distinguished service in wartime, and he attributes much of his success to what he learned from others, both at sea and in his earlier days in his home town of Stromness.)

Growing up in Stromness, we enjoyed a freedom which sadly is denied our young today. When the snow fell we could sledge from Oglaby to Cooper's Garage or via the Crescent to Leslie's Close. We could clog in the Manse Park, Castle Park, the Crescent or Franklin Road. We could play rounders in the Square and football wherever there was a space. We had our mis-spent youth facilities, our further education centres – the billiard halls, the bakehouses and Peter Esson's tailor shop where we acquired counting skills playing pontoon for matches. We had the Cattle Shed for 'pitch and toss' and the Apostolic Church Hall for our Sunday evening entertainment.

Winter meant visiting trawlers, either storm-bound or requiring bunkers or repairs. Our long serving Harbourmaster, James Harvey, always in attendance, once told a Grimsby trawler skipper to 'splash astern,' to which he replied 'I have been going astern all my life otherwise I wouldn't be here.' Needless to say, the nickname remained 'Splash.' James, however, did the job singlehanded. He cleaned the shed, swept the piers, lit the Leading Lights, moored the ships, kept the books in immaculate order and supplied us with the booty received from the relatively wealthy trawler skippers. Many a fisherman got trawl twine to make his creel-covers, hungry youngsters their only real good meals from the galley, together with cigarette shag and tins of humbugs from the crew.

When wireless was in its infancy at sea and not yet compulsory, one such trawler arrived in Stromness in the hope of getting the wireless repaired. John Isbister, known to be a wireless enthusiast, was summoned. He succeeded in getting the wireless working. When asked the charge, he replied 'Och, I only want five bob for doing the job but I want £5 for knowing what to do!' A real lesson in the value of skill!

During the thirties, the *Skarv*, *Taylor*, *Tayson* or *Argentum* would bring coal to Sutherland's pier, and the *Edenside* or *Fernside* to the opposition. The *Dennis* or *Denwick Head* would go to the Pole Star Pier, and the *St. Fergus* or *St. Clement* to the Ola Pier, known as the 'Warehouse Pier.' I had complete access to the vessels lying at Sutherland's and the Pole Star Pier. Long before I got geometry at school, the skipper of the *Dennis Head* taught me how to bisect a line and position a ship with cross bearings. The Fishery Cruisers were viewed but never boarded; the officers wore gold braid!

Sailing, boating and swimming (dipping, as we termed it) gave us real outlet for our energies. The weather never seemed to stop us. We considered the sea was always warmer during the rain when we would use the lifeboat slip. At lunchtime or at 4 o' clock, we would use Clouston's Pier or swing on the crane at Sutherland's Pier and drop off when clear of the pier. At 6 pm on a Sunday, we would go off the 'New Pier' or the top of the wheelhouse of the *Hoy Head*. Although we could not swim well, we made the ladder by 'doggie paddle.'

Our first experience of sailing was by rowing to the mouth of the harbour, hoisting a sackcloth sail, and sailing down-wind. We graduated to being ballast or required to bail out; then to jibsheets and ultimately the tiller – a long apprenticeship. The critics, the old retired seamen, lined up on the piers watching our performances, and if we misbehaved, they would soon sort us out. Our learning was achieved by imitation and correction.

Tuesday night was Points Racing; which was always re-run at the Pier Head and generally ended in argument. By listening ,we were learning the rules. Regatta Day started with the waterline being measured at Clouston's Slip, and ballast could not be changed thereafter. During the evening, the presentation of trophies took place in the Town Hall and a dance followed. The filling of the cups provided the second opportunity of the year to imbibe. When the dance started, we peeped through the windows.

Any visiting yacht could be sure of a welcome when anchored in the harbour. Flatties or dinghies emerged from all the slipways and an armada surrounded them. Occasionally, a larger yacht would anchor in Cairston Roads and only the enthusiasts would apply the effort to go that far.

Our only bus trip was the Sunday School Picnic or a specially-hired trip to Kirkwall for the Inter-County football and hockey or the County Show; not both. We did have a motor-boat picnic to Pegal Burn or Longhope, provided a number contributed to the cost. We were thankful for small mercies. Most of us worked for our pennies. I pumped the church organ and this bought my clothes. I carried coal at a young age and was very proud to hand over my pay to my mother who slaved to feed and clothe us. As youngsters, we helped each other. We were reared to work, to be honest; independent and sympathetic. We were exposed to all the frailties. Stromness had its fair share of available girls and ladies, willing men and visiting seamen. It happily accommodated the unfortunates in society which today would be sent to institutions. We had our delightful characters whom we fondly remember and who brightened our lives.

Titty Bell, the provider of immaculately clean washing, would drop her basket in the Square, lift her skirts, and give us a jog. Ally Harvey, 'Whap,' when asked by a minister if he had a message for his brother, said yes, 'Tell him it's a long way to Tipperary.' The unsuspecting minister did not realise the brothers had not spoken for over 30 years!

There was Tully who rolled through the street as if he owned it. He was oblivious to the cars, and when pulled to the side just in time to avoid one, he protested, 'Did he blaw?' To which the reply was: 'You're damn lucky you didn't hear Gabriel's horn blowing!'

His brother Davick maintained that he knew each trawler's home port by the shade of the smoke.

Stromness must also remember those who did so much for so little – such as the late Provost George Robertson – 'Doddie,' as he was affectionately known. He encouraged us young ones to contribute. His efforts produced the bather sheleter at the 'Tender Tables' at the West Shore, very useful in tis day, the original tennis court, the Golf Course, the Market green, and later the Community Centre, and all manner of ploys to give the young constructive activity. His example has been partially emulated buy others but never surpassed.

Looking back, I was sea-orientated from childhood, and this little town thrived on its association with the sea. As young boys, our heroes were the seafarers; we listened intently and open-mouthed to the tales of the sea and exotic foreign lands. The numerous retired and serving shipmasters, smartly attired, dwelling in smart houses, named after the ships they commanded, or the foreign places which had attracted them, were examples to be emulated. Many of these masters gave the young of the town their start in seafaring and others such as myself an ambition to become one of them.

October 1995

STROMNESS – 70 YEARS AGO

JACKIE BROWN

(When Jackie Brown was the manager of the Bank of Scotland in Stromness, the bankhouse became at times of year like New Year and Stromness Shopping Week a joyous meeting-place for all ages. There you would find a wonderful mixture of people and stories and music and laughter, all gathered together through the great delight taken by Jackie and his wife, Maria, in humanity in all its diversity. There would be farmers from the country, fishermen with stories of the islands, well-known Stromness characters, or writers and poets who had come to visit Jackie's younger brother, George Mackay Brown. Amidst the warmth of the hospitality, the stories would flow, and some of the classic themes were accounts of older Stromness. After retirement from the bank and subsequent service as Orkney Islands Councillor for Birsay, Jackie is now writing down some of his reminiscences of the town and its people.)

Seventy years ago, the mile-long street, in contrast to the present, was devoid of traffic. John Mackay of the Stromness Hotel owned the first car and Mr Bain of the Mason's Arms Hotel had two cars for hire, while Robert Nicolson ran the daily bus between Kirkwall and Stromness. The witty and incorrigible Danny Watt delivered heavy goods in his horse-drawn lorry. So the street and the closes and the piers belonged to the children of the town. Here we played our football and here the boys and girls would indulge in boisterous games.

And the piers, twenty or so, were not very far from the street; they were the places of enchantment. Here the many fishermen, line fishermen in their twenty-foot motorised yawls would be preparing for sea and baiting their longlines. Here we could borrow their dinghies or flatties to row into the harbour or cross over to the two small islands, the Inner and Outer Holms, across the bay.

Life in the town went on at a leisurely pace. Where my family lived, in the centre, were three meeting-places where men could pop in for a yarn. Peter Esson's tailor shop, Bill Mathieson's saddlery shop and Geordie Linklater's ship chandler's shop – all within 25 yards of each other. As a small boy Peter Esson's tailor shop was a fascinating place for me, an enchanted place where my small world broadened and was enlivened by stories from exotic places.

Inside the door and at right angles to the street was a broad bench where Peter could cut the cloth for his suits and where he could, with his heavy iron, press them when finished. And on this bench, when not in use by Peter, they would sit, legs dangling for the bench was high, the exclusive club of citizens who daily frequented the place. All were elderly and, like many Orcadians, had travelled to far-off places as sailors or as emigrants and, while not discussing local gossip, they would reminisce on incidents and adventures abroad.

Peter also was a wonderful storyteller with a remarkable memory for dates and events that had happened locally. I would listen, fascinated. Although he had been in the 1914-18 war he rarely spoke about it; probably the memory was too poignant. I remember him saying, 'I do not know how we survived. I think we lived on fresh air.'

Peter was also the town librarian and lived above the library which still exists at the foot of Hellihole Road. People would drop in the tailor's shop to collect the papers and magazines they had purchased at the half yearly library auction. But his greatest love was the kirk, the United Free Church of Scotland, of which he was an elder. Of the minister, the Rev. James Christie, he spoke in awe as if he was a latter-day saint. My brother, George, seven years younger than me, also had the same fascination for the shop and when Peter died at the age of 70 felt compelled to write the poem: 'The Death of Peter Esson – Tailor, Town Librarian, Free Kirk Elder.' This sonnet, so beautifully constructed, echoed all my memories. The Free Kirk, now the Town Hall, climbed steeply up the close beside

Peter's shop, looking down on it from its steepled height – triumphant!

Peter always spoke of his minister as 'Mister Christie' but when he spoke of our minister, the Rev. Muirhead, of the United Presbyterian Church of Scotland, it was always 'Muirhead did this and that,' in a demeaning fashion. This reflected the rivalry in the town between the three main churches. This no longer applies as there is only one Presbyterian church now in Stromness. The Old or Established Church of Scotland is the present-day Community Centre.

South from the tailor's shop and separated by the close that leads up to the Free Kirk was the saddler's shop where Bill Mathieson applied his trade. This was another fascinating place which had its own coterie of gossipers. It also had its own special smell of leather and resin and here Bill plied his needle and resined thread in rhythmic fashion on a saddle or a girth or a pupil's schoolbag. On one occasion Bill came to my rescue after an accident playing football. I had got a bad kick from a boys' iron-shod boot which refused to heal. It was painful and angry. However Bill had the answer. He made a pad of soft leather on which he placed hot resin in the shape of a patch. It did the trick, drawing out all the pus, and in no time it was healed. I still have the mark as evidence.

A few yards south along the street and on the other side was the ship chandler's shop of Geordie Linklater. It had its own special clientele and its own special aroma of rope, tar, apples. This clientele were the sea captains of the town, mostly retired, and other sea-going personnel. Stromness had a goodly number of sea captains, among them the three Ritch brothers who came originally from the island of Graemsay – Captain George, Captain John and Captain Magnus. Then there were the two Captains John Sinclair, father and son from the Whitehouse (once visited by Captain Bligh of the *Bounty*) and Captain Flett of Ness House.

Geordie Linklater, a small man with a distinctive limp, always made the point of purchasing *Lloyds Gazette* at the auction of periodicals at the library. Produced by Lloyds of London, it showed where all the British ships were at any given time and, of course, this interested the shipmasters. The three Ritch brothers were skippers in the King Line, and Geordie could tell Captain Magnus that the *King James* was three days out of Boston on the 23rd.

In the town there were quite a number of very small shops where widowed women eked out a livelihood selling sweats and lemonade. One of those possessed the colourful name of Ginger Beery Babbie. Her little shop, part of her house, lay tucked in between the Bank of Scotland and Rae's paper shop. She was the aunt of the infamous James Leask, the bellman, universally known as 'Puffer,' who lived further south along the street and up one of the many closes. Although five or six families lived up the close, it was called 'Puffer's Close.' Puffer was slightly lame and had to use a stick. As he walked along the street, he would puff and blow quite audibly. As youngsters we were rather afraid of him. When he was standing on a corner he would attempt to trip us with his stick as we ran along, so we would avoid him. Looking back, I think it was all part of a game with no evil intent. However there was a cruel streak in his nature. When Puffer's mother died his aunt, Ginger Beery Babbie, attended the funeral in the house up the close. Apparently his aunt was keening loudly during the service when Puffer was heard to say in a loud whisper, 'Will someone not give her a kick in the shins?'

Another character of repute was 'Soldier John' – John Johnston, the town crier and verger of the Episcopal Church of Scotland, a small chapel up the Church Road. He had been the town crier before Puffer and had been a foot soldier with General Gordon in India about which he loved to expand. He was frequently heard to expound in Bill Matheson's saddlery shop and his stories about India were treated with suspicion – and sometimes derision. He had a deep sonorous voice, admirable for a town crier and admirable for his stories. On one occasion when he concluded with 'I have stood where thousands fell,' a wit, Sam Stockan, quickly said 'Thousands of lice, Jeck.'

In Peter Esson's shop it was suggested to Soldier John that the townsfolk would enjoy a talk on 'India,' and that he could charge a silver collection. The Temperance Hall was filled to capacity; this should be a memorable occasion. In his rich and loud voice Soldier John commenced, 'In India some worship the sun, some worship the moon and some worship the Brahmaputra hen. Many's the time when I have seen a woman throw her child into the jaws of an alligator.' Loud cheers from the audience, and that was just the beginning.

Other characters roamed the street and piers of Stromness. Geordie Chalmers thought he was a ship. Dressed in a reifer jacket with brass buttons and cheesecutter cap, he walked along muttering 'starboard' or 'port' or 'a splash astern.' When asked why he had walked the ten miles to Dounby on a windy day, his answer was, 'to get a back wind home.'

Then there was James Miller who would stroll slowly down the pier clutching at the chain of his pocket watch, and suddenly explode with the most unusual expression 'crunch a halibut.' And that was how he was called; sometimes abbreviated to 'Crunch.' Both he and Geordie Chalmers were quite innocuous and just part of the scene.

It was a grand place in which to grow up.

October 1995

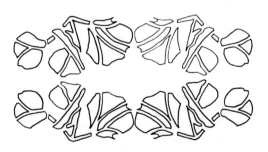

'PUFFER'

GEORGE S. ROBERTSON

(Ex-Provost George S. Robertson was one of the most remarkable men of his generation, with a single-minded belief in the common good that led him to inspire the community to undertake many large projects by sheer hard work and enthusiasm. He was born in Sanday in 1887, his family later moving to Westray, and then Stromness where George worked for many years in the Post Office. After long and distinguished service in local government, he could still, when in his 90's, go round the Stromness golf course in less than his age. His vision for the community was combined with a deep understanding of his fellow-men, of whom he could recount many stories.)

A previous generation of Stromnessians knew James Leask ('Puffer') as a man, the present generation only as a hearsay. I first made his acquaintance in 1900, the year I came to Stromness. Previously, he had been twice in prison for assaults. We heard the usual tales from the prison. At one court Puffer feigned deafness. The Sheriff said, 'Leask, you are no deafer than any one in this court. We will read the charge over once more, that you assaulted Thomas Smith, and you must either say you are guilty or not guilty.' James said: 'Me?? I've never driven a motor car in my life!' A typical Pufferism.

The tailor's wife asked James to weed her vegetable garden. He set to and pulled up every vegetable, leaving only the weeds. She was not even angry. She said, 'I'm sorry for the poor man. He's so stupid.'

In Stromness there was a Salvation Army station in what is now the Lifeboat house. At a testimony meeting, James professed a religious life, and that he had been a missionary in China for a period. 'Praise the Lord!' said the Salvationist,

'Would you come to another meeting and give us more news of your work?' He promised he would. Some days later, the Salvationist was down the pier when cattle were being loaded on a steamer, and she reported to the meeting that she 'witnessed our erstwhile missionary twisting the tail of a bullock.'

Young people were afraid of Puffer. He threatened them with his stick, but he did not actually molest them. In 1915 Puffer was expelled from Stromness as an undesirable citizen, and he went to Musselburgh, and worked in the goods yard on the railway station. He was on visiting terms with a Mr Smith, who lived in Musselburgh and had a factory in Prestonpans. His wife was a Stromness woman, and this fact may account for Puffer being in Musselburgh.

Some months later, I returned to Musselburgh, and contacted James. I suggested to him that he should come to the morning services with me. He agreed, and he never missed once in the six months before I joined the Army. I took him to the Hibs matches at Easter Road on the Saturday, and once we went to the Ibrox match in Glasgow. He wrote to someone in Stromness saying that George Robertson and he had been at a sixty-thousand match and when we entered all the men on the terraces stood up in our honour.

One day on the High Street, I saw James standing outside a public house, obviously drunk and incapable. I took his arm and said, 'I'll take you home, Jimmy.' He came and never said a word, and never referred to his condition. The following day, which was a Saturday, he told Smith what had happened, and Smith said: 'Robertson will have nothing more to do with you after that. And when I came out of my digs on Sunday morning, Jimmy was waiting outside on the street. After the service, we strolled down to the golf course, which was also the Edinburgh racecourse. I never mentioned the Friday episode, and I could sense that James was relieved.

James returned to Stromness after the Armistice, and got in no trouble with the police. The King was ill, and Buckingham Palace issued a daily report. James followed suit, for his mild indisposition, placing in his window every morning the progress of his condition. 'Had a good night, and slept some hours. If this progress continues, I shall be able soon to resume my bellman duties.'

Regarding his calls, he often added something unconnected with it, calculated to raise a laugh.

The chief constable in Musselburgh told me one day: 'We had your friend Leash or Leask in for being in possession of a bottle of spirits without the vendor's name. Leask said, 'Do you know a pub in Tranent, with a pump in the back garden?' I replied, 'Yes.' 'Well, you can pump that. You're not going to pump me.' We thought he was not all there, so we let him out.'

Finally, James in feeble health was sent to the County Home. There, to prevent him working any of his pranks, he was kept in bed. I visited him once, and found him lying next to Soldier John, and shortly thereafter they both passed on.

BBC Radio Orkney recording

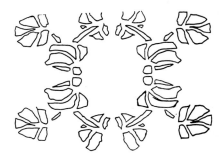

BOOTS SHOES & BENDS

FIONA MACINNES

(A member of the hugely talented MacInnes family, Fiona has all the skills of an artist and a writer, combined with a fiercely honest self-criticism that leads her to rewrite and pare down until she feels that the final form has been reached. She lives in Stromness with her husband, Neil Matheson, and teaches. Her commitment to society made her for a while an Islands Councillor, where her articulateness and compassion and determination for justice was demonstrated fully. She can, in the words of George Mackay Brown introducing her first book of poems, To Step Among Wrack, 'sketch a landscape with a few vivid words.' Here now is a poem from the next one.)

Boots Shoes & Bends
Is what it says on the end
Of Mr Wright's Shop

You squeeze in sideways
And the bell goes ping
He has always been very
Very old

He has a little hat
Like a saucer on his head
Behind the big sewing machine
Swirly black gold

He hammers on heels
And stitches on soles
Then to make sure
He nails them all too

I will never know how the nails in the soles
Don't get stuck in your toe
But then
There you go!

Waiting to be mended next
Are rows and rows of shoes on shelves
Tatty scuffed or down at heel
They soon will all be good as new

When last year's boots have got too small
It's down to Mr Wright's we go
From small to big they're all on show
Ready waiting for the snow

Rubber boots
With sizes chalked
Jump and stamp
Make room for socks

The parcel then is all made up
In sheets of paper noisy brown
With string and slip knots
Tightly pulled
The money clinks
Inside the till
And with our booty off we go

Down the street
And up the hill…

MEMORIES OF ROBERT SHAW

ARCHIE BEVAN

(Archie Bevan is a master of just about every aspect of the craft of using words, from literary criticism to reading for radio or stage with his wife Elizabeth. He has enriched Orkney cultural life immensely, from his teaching days at Stromness Academy, where he pioneered the study of Orkney writers, to his major role in St Magnus Festival's development. This Radio Orkney recording was broadcast in 1978.)

I think Robert Shaw would have been about seven years old when he first came to Orkney in the early 1930's. The family settled in Stromness when his father set up his medical practice in the town. They lived in Seafield House, opposite the Bank of Scotland, the house from which Dr Cromarty later ran his medical practice for many years.

The Shaws were a lively family. Dr Shaw himself was a great outdoor man, fond of shooting and fishing, and something of a *bon vivant* – at least by the douce Orcadian standards of those days.

Robert was two classes below me in school, an unbridgeable gulf at that age. But he was a classmate and companion of my cousin, Captain Arthur Porteous.

His schooldays in Stromness made an enduring impression on Robert Shaw. When I met him again more than twenty years later, he recalled those days in vivid detail. He was able to name his classroom friends – and enemies – and he remembered the bitterness he had felt in the early days when he was ganged up on by a small clique – headed, not by an Orcadian, but by an incomer like himself.

Those childhood years were not a tale of unbroken delight for Robert Shaw. Much later in his life he was able to recapture the joy, and the anguish, of his Stromness days in some vivid semi-autobiographical writing in his first two novels – *The Hiding Place* and *The Sun Doctor.*

The family left Stromness just before or after the start of the War. It was 1960 before Robert Shaw returned to Orkney on holiday. By this time he had established a considerable reputation on the London stage. He had just begun his career in the popular cinema with a smallish part in *The Dam Busters.* He had already made his mark on TV with a starring role in a series called, I believe, *The Buccaneers,* but this was before the advent of TV in Orkney. He had already published his first novel, The Hiding Place, a work of high promise. He was busy writing his second novel, and he told me that he had no less than seven more books mapped out in his head.

He returned to Orkney in the summer of 1963 with his second wife, Mary Ure, the Scottish actress who had made her name as the long-suffering wife in John Osborne's play *Look back in Anger.* I remember that my first meeting with Robert Shaw that year was on the Stromness Golf Course. He was playing in a foursome with some members of the local club – partnering Jim Sutherland, I think. His dark hair had been bleached to a startline Aryan blond, a remnant of his starring role as the villain in *From Russia with Love,* which he had just finished shooting. Of course, you'll remember that he came to a sticky end, at the hands of James Bond, in that film, but Shaw told me that in fact he and Sean Connery were very close friends, and he had a great admiration for Connery's ability as an actor.

Incidentally, it was on one of those Orkney holidays that the nursemaid to the Shaw family met, and in due course married, Mr George Brown, son of the late Ginger Brown.

My most vivid memory of Robert Shaw that summer was a visit we paid to Rackwick. My family was camping in Hoy that year, and we gave the Shaws a lift through from Lyness. As we turned in to the valley under the shadow of the Ward Hill and the Dwarfie Hamars, Robert Shaw enthralled the youngsters in the car by launching into a delightful story featuring the Trow of Trowieglen. He was a born storyteller, with a great imaginative gift and a wonderful way with words.

He left Orkney shortly afterwards and I never saw him again. His performance in *From Russia with Love* set him on a road to stardom, which was to culminate in blockbusters like *The Battle of the Bulge, Jaws* and *The Deep*, though some of his finest films never achieved box-office success.

But his great aim back in 1963 was to be a successful writer. And for a time at least it seemed that the promise of that first novel would be abundantly fulfilled. His second book, *The Sun Doctor*, was generally acclaimed, and won the Hawthornden Prize. It is in fact a rather uneven book, but it does have an autobiographical flavour in certain parts, particularly in his account of the hero's return to Orkney to discover the truth of his childhood experience in the islands.

Shaw wrote three more books, including *The Man in the Glass Booth*, which later became a successful stage play. But for my money, his finest achievement was undoubtedly his third novel, *The Flag*, a work of great imaginative power. This book was to have been the first of a trilogy of novels, and Shaw's admirers waited long and hopefully for the second instalment. Alas, we waited in vain.

Robert Shaw went on to become a superstar in the cinema, but he never quite fulfilled his promise as a writer. I do not know whether the trilogy would ever have been completed, but the fact that these books remained unwritten certainly added to the sense of loss which I shared with all his Stromness friends at the news of his sudden death last week.

BBC Radio Orkney recording, August 3rd 1978

NECESSARY MAGIC

MORAG MCGILL

(And now for another member of the MacInnes family. A sister of Fiona, Morag lives with her husband, John McGill, in Lincoln, where both do much freelance writing. She is highly versatile, but for a while has been working in between other commitments on a book of stories about Stromness, focused particularly on the town's annual Shopping Week, established in 1949 to counter post-war decline. The Week took its names from the shops who worked together to set it up, but in the eyes of a generation or two of young Orcadians who flock annually from all parts to join in the celebrations, it is something of an annual carnival to turn a quiet summer into a time of excitement and adventure – as this story shows.)

The thing about Shopping Week was that you grew up to it. Or through it. Or despite it, or because of it. Whether you were seven, waving your pirate knife at the judges to impress them, or seventeen and impressing even severer judges while dancing to the Alphabeats at the Town Hall, it was a testing time. Of course, it was always summer, and the appearance of that duster yellow programme in Rae's, print dancing over it red as happiness, guaranteed holiday time, and fireworks, and strange pipe bands. School was over, and the Showies were at the Market Green. There were visitors in town, folk who might have been Orcadian once, but whose voices had taken on other, foreign cadences; you all crowded the pier to identify them as they stumbled off the Saturday boat to the bellowing of seasick bulls. There were Events – and such events! Fire eaters and tightrope walkers and Wall of Death riders! From the moment Aubrey turned the corner of Eric Flett's, leading the horses all plaited and beribboned, he gleaming with pride and anxiety just as much as they, coaxing them past the pierhead fountain to wait for the lifeboat bringing the Queen to be crowned – from that moment anything could happen – fun was allowed. It was put in a yellow Programme. It was timetabled (in the Town Hall if wet). Even the teachers could have some fun, if they chose. Even Mr Groundwater, who was about ten feet tall and grave as a Bible story.

But if it had just been fun, Shopping Week wouldn't have much hold on the heart. Testing, I said it was. You remember the tests, and the pain of failing them. Or passing.

At first it was simple things. Remember shaking and swaying in that old lorry with the great round hump of radiator at the front, that domestic, homely fifties shape, on your way to the Fancy Dress Parade? Jumbled up tight against Minnie Mouse, several princesses, Robin Hood and the Beverley Sisters, trying to keep the sharn off the painted sheet that was turning you into somebody not yourself, a scary Dressed Up person? Your feet slipped on the wet green floor (lorries were scarce, and a quick hose down was all they got). Off you went, shaking and swaying, to the clank of the tailgate and the skirl of the pipes in front and the fiddle and accordion behind – and this great glob of excitement rose in you, and the crowd all yelled and threw pennies – and one caught you, right sore, in the corner of the eye. And you couldn't even cry because the paint on your sheet would run.

Remember worrying if you'd win the money and hoping she'd pick you, this dressy Queen with her crown and stiff hair who drove about in a gold cart in the rain smiling? This Queen who usually lived in a Palace in London with Beefeaters and men in Bearskins on guard? Which you knew because Miss Merriman had told you in school. It was on the page next to the Pygmies in the geography book, beside the red map of the Empire. She was definitely an important Queen; they got the lifeboat out for her.

Remember parading round in the mud and waiting for hours and watching all the Young Farmers dressed as women losing the balloons in their dresses and roaring and peeing behind the goal posts when they though nobody was watching?

And after all that, you didn't get the red and yellow rosette – and you didn't hear who did because the two big loudspeakers on top of the judging car in the middle of the field were pointing in the wrong direction, and the wind was carrying the winners' names to America. So nobody was sure until Carol Christie's mother pulled her out to the front, her again, she wins every year, her mother sends to London for material. That would have been OK, because you had been well schooled – it's not the winning, it's the taking part that matters, they said, teachers and parents and all – stupid, when it would have meant money to spend on Tobermory tatties and sweetie bracelets and lucky bags and everlasting strips and sweetie cigarettes and bottles of Mowatt's orange lemonade with the bits in the bottom and the swoosh of gas at the top... – but then Edna Burgess said it wasn't the real Queen because it was her big sister's best friend dressed up and she'd never been out of Dounby, let alone lived in London in a Palace with Bears. The real Queen was that one who came when you had to polish your uniform belt and your lace-up shoes, and she had a rain mate on and not a gold cart in sight, or a velvet cloak. Pain and betrayal!

Then of course came the year when suddenly none of it was satisfactory, not the roll-a-penny stall with its clutch of goldfish in plastic bags swinging in the wind; not the mysterious coconuts, hard as heads but sloppy when you shook them; not the great trek out to the Market Green to see the Main Attraction, miles above you, unicyclists in tights wobbling into gusts of weather, braver than anybody realised, three times a week and twice on Saturday. Somehow it all seemed too tame for you. You knew the Queen. You hadn't voted for her, but there she was under some plastic awning breathing hard, still hot from the dryer, got up like somebody twice her age in a bouffant backcombed style; looking suddenly just like the Monday cake in the bakery, modest but overdressed and a bit embarrassed, sitting in a doily. You wanted something more; competitions with bigger prizes.

So. Remember the noise from the Town Hall, the palm wetting thud of the bass? Remember the cardboard box of

EP's upstairs in Jackie Tait's? (If you break You Pay, written everywhere in the new blue Biro pen you could try out at the glass counter.) Oh, those magic words – EMI, DECCA, 45rpm; those orange stripy paper sleeves with 7/6 on them, those shiny pictures of Dusty Springfield, looking like an angel with black eyes and white lips! You had to get your hair cut over your eyes like Ringo and buy a white nylon polo neck from Kirkwall; you had to get boots with Cuban heels. The only place to get Panstick was Woolies, and you had to lagger it all over your neck as well as your face so it covered you with a Californian tan. You went to Raymie's cafe and drank frothy coffee out of see-through cups and saucers; you hung around waiting for something. Or somebody. Waiting to be picked, to get a rosette.

You were too young to drink but they said if you took vodka nobody smelt it. You negotiated like a Trojan to get out to the best dances, the ones with the highest danger tariff – Wednesday because it was Young Farmers, Saturday because it was the Last Night. Boys wanted to be in the football match, to beat the Kirkwall Starlings or the snobby kiltie cadets from Gordonstoun and Dunblane; girls wanted to watch, to be on the corner just as the pipe band passed, to yell from the touchline; to get noticed by the wonderful, glamorous kiltie cadets.

You were all there, remember? You all walked the empty streets in the drizzle with a friend, hoping to be overtaken before you got home, before the bus came, before the cafe shut, by an adventure.

And then it happened, probably the year after you'd decided Shopping Week was rubbish. The prize came your way. Didn't you get off with somebody, somebody not Orcadian, some girl from Arbroath, up on her holidays, with real stiletto heels? Some boy from Skye or Edinburgh or Rotherham, smelling of Old Spice and wet corduroy? Remember, you met on the Tuesday, you held hands on the Wednesday at the Baby Show and then in the damp grey light after the football you walked all round the Tender Tables in the rain with the sea quietly lapping; maybe you sat in a lump of wartime concrete and kissed, or went too far in the back of somebody's car and worried for three weeks, I can't be sure. Whatever happened, you fell in love and bought a pendant with a leather thong, or a Stromness keyring, or you won a fluffy monkey on elastic shooting at pitted targets with a stiff old gun. You might have it yet, if you take a look, somewhere in the attic.

At the end of Shopping Week you waved goodbye to the Ola, with the piper's melancholy, hungover howl in your ears, and you wrote a couple of letters; you traced names out in kisses and wrote SWALK across the back of the envelopes. And then school started and you forgot about it, sort of, except that you'd negotiated another test, for better or worse – started off on another journey.

And you'd never believed, would you, if they told you then, that some day you'd choose not to go down and see the crowning; that the fireworks might suddenly seem less than a mystical magical show that lasted forever, and more like a lot of noise just when you'd got the bairn settled; that the gaiety, the noise, the exuberance on the streets might look more like a drunken ruckus; that you'd notice the broken bottles and the spew more than the beat of the music? Just like you never thought about how it came about, who made it, who was in charge. Just like you'd never have believed that one year, on summer, it might not happen. Just like you didn't believe you'd get old.

You took it like a gift, didn't you – necessary magic, wrapped by the town in a red and yellow programme. Experience free. (In the Town Hall if wet.)

SILLOCKS AND CUITHES

CAPT. JOHN GRAY

(Captain John Gray comes from Papa Westray, and in his early years at sea went to the Baltic and to South Georgia with Salvesens. After a period on coasters and on the North boats, he joined Captain John Hourie in providing the shipping service to the South Isles. He has many memories of his boyhood in the North Isles, here describing the great Orcadian pastime of catching sillocks and going to the cuithes.)

'Sillocks' and 'cuithes' are really young coalfish, but when they reach maturity they go by the name of *saithe*. Their flesh is not so white as cod or haddock but when salted and dried (generally air-dried on the beaches or on the roofs of outhouses), they are very good to eat. In the harvest time the waters round our shores are usually just alive with so many of these little fishes. Cuithes are usually a bit smaller in size than a herring, whilst a sillock is about half that size, being a season younger.

To catch them, you generally have to try and fish where the sea water is moving fairly fast, such as in a roost or röst between islands, and around about harvest time is when they are most numerous. These little fishes when they are at that age are excellent eating; you gut and clean them and remove the head and the tail, then cover them with the white of an egg and roll them in oatmeal or in beremeal and fry them in a pan with some bacon or pork fat. Do not try to turn the fish in the pan until they have stiffened somewhat, otherwise they will all go crumbly and you will have to sup them up with a spoon. Fried in this way with pepper and salt you have a delicious meal, especially if you have mealy tatties and butter fat to eat with it.

To catch them you have rods, or wands as we call them, each with a line of about eight feet in length and a cast of three flies using white hen or gull feathers fastened into the gut or nylon with a barbed hook on each. You troll the flies at the stern of your little boat, and if the fish are in the mood you will be kept busy.

In our young days in the islands, salted cuithes was the main diet. They would have been cleaned and salted and air-dried on the roofs of outhouses, then to finish them you bundled several together by their tails and hung them in the roof of your kitchen, where there was a moving warm air, and let them hang there for several weeks. By that time the salt on their outside would be glittering in the lamp light like sugar, and then they were just right for eating. For a meal you soaked them in water and boiled them for a little while to soften the flesh, then ate them with mealy tatties and butter fat – an excellent meal that one never failed to enjoy.

I well remember the first time that I went off to catch cuithes. I would have been about five years old or so. My old grandad asked me if I would come off in his little boat with him and with someone to row the boat. This little boat was always called the Sow (soo), why I do not know. Anyhow I was all excited to think that I would be able to fish for cuithes. At the big farmhouse of Holland in Papay they had quite a large garden where, among other things, they grew mint and myrrh, and also honeysuckle, and in the evening when the fish would be taking, the sweet scent would waft its way down across where we would be trolling. It was really beautiful and I can never forget this, no more than I can my first adventure at the cuithes.

I was given a rod or wand. It would have been about eight feet long, and the line and its cast of flies another eight feet. You laid it out over the stern of the dinghy and sat on it on the seat. When a fish takes a hold, he will jerk away as best he can to get clear of the hook. Now old Grandad was a whiskery old man, and not very tolerant either towards us young fellows who sometimes spoke as if we knew everything! You need a certain amount of expertise to really know how to get a hooked cuithe safely into the boat. For one thing you must never let him come out of the water until you have him close to the stern, otherwise he will keep jerking, causing the line with him attached to swing round and round the wand. In this instance and in my excitement I forgot the rules, and as soon as the fish took the hook I jerked the rod right out of the water. Consequently it started to swing round and round with the jerking fish on the end of the line, and eventually came around old Grandad's head and my own as well.

Then unfortunately the hook caught in old Grandad's lug and with the fish jerking away it soon went through the soft part of his lug.

Boy-oh-boy, did he not yell and call me all sorts of names for being such a stupid nut. In the long run we had to go to the shore with him, for he got so mad with the pain of the jerking fish and the blood pouring down his face. Then we got my Dad to come with his pliers and cut the hook so that we could withdraw it backwards from its barb.

But it was a long time before he asked me back again to be a hand in his little fishing boat – although his wound was not so serious, and he soon recovered after he had a pan of fried sillocks with his tea.

BBC Radio Orkney (1987)

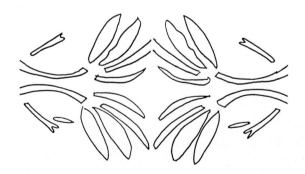

SUMMER SOUNDS IN STRONSAY

TOM MCLACHLAN

(Orcadian exiles often recall in clear detail aspects of Orkney which are fading from memory. Tom McLachlan, who came from Stronsay, used to contribute vivid pictures of the days of the herring fishing, when the boats packed into the harbour at the village in Whitehall and the sounds of activity carried along the shore.)

Whenever the wind was strong there was always the slapping of halyards against the masts of the sailing boats. The sound was like the continuous cracking of gigantic whips, for the masts were at least sixty feet high, and the manilla halyards were one and a half inches in diameter. When upwards of a hundred boats were tied up at the pier, one would think from the constant slapping of ropes against wood that the Devil himself was lashing about him with tempestuous fury.

The groaning and crunching of wood fenders, as these were crushed between the boats, or the boats themselves bruising and chafing the great greenheart fenders of the pier, sounded as if living things were in pain. Perhaps the most lonely and saddest sound of all was the wild howling in the rigging of ships. This was to be heard on the smacks which carried mainstays and ratlines as did most of the cargo steamers. It was easy then to imagine that spirits ruled the wind and rode the storms.

While all this mad music of the wind was in full blast, the light-gliding sea-gulls screamed their demoniacal cries. These sounds would be heard for days at a time and in high summer too, for the fishing fleet only came to our village in summer time. Then suddenly the wind would die down and the quietness of a northern isle could be felt.

The sea along the pier while the wind had been at its height made little or no noise, for the large number of boats riding on its surface acted as oil does on troubled waters. Only when the boats had put to sea after the summer storm, the gentle lapping of the waves on shingle could be heard. Now and again a sudden movement could be seen in the calm water, and a medium sized wave would rush, hissing shorewards the length of the pier, to finish up with a resounding slap on the beach. This phenomenon always surprised old and young alike as there was no accounting for it. Were there spirits in the deep?

Often as not after a summer storm the islands were wrapped in impenetrable white fog. Then could be heard the hand operated fog-horns of the sailing boats. These instruments were about two feet six inches long and four inches in diameter. They were made telescopic-like. The operator pulled one piece out as far as possible then slowly shoved it back again. The resulting sound was like the bellowing of a maddened bull and could be heard at a very considerable distance. Between the monotonous groans of the fog-horns could be heard the creaking of row-locks as fishermen plied the long sweeps to help make progress in the almost flat calm – and perhaps a snatch of some sea chanty whistled by a tired fisherman coaxing a fresh wind to blow.

When steam or sailing drifters eventually reached the pier after a night at sea, there came a time of indescribable confusion and noise. Over a hundred vessels at a time were all trying to get a berth at a pier that couldn't accommodate fifty. The Harbour Master shouted and swore at skippers who had thrown mooring lines ashore, hoopla fashion, so that the loop or bite landed over the mooring posts. To drown his cries the drifter skippers blew piercing blasts on their sirens. The Harbour Master or his assistants would then cut away the mooring ropes with stout axes so that a vessel couldn't warp herself up to the head of the queue, so to speak.

When the herring began to be unloaded there was the constant snickering sound of all kinds of block and tackle in action. There was the hissing of steam from capstans and boilers, from steam drifters and sailing boats alike. The latter all had boilers and capstans to help hoist sail, shoot nets, and haul, as well as load and unload cargo.

Amidst this din, young fish salesmen tried to make their voices heard. Some of them were students on vacation, earning a bit of money to eke out their bursaries. They were quick and alert but got no better prices sometimes than one or two, who, bearded like the bard, kept up a slow soft monotone. "Saxteen an' sax gentlemen for a cran, Saxteen an' sax; Seeventeen shullings then, Seeventeen shullings – Seeventeen an' sax, Thank ye gentlemen Auchteen shullings it is...."

In the long summer days when the sun shone out of a cloudless blue sky, and the fishing fleet were still at sea, there were sounds to be heard in the village which were muted by distance. The tap -tapping sounds of coopers knocking on hoops of herring barrels came faintly along the beach and often the snatches of Gaelic songs sung by West Highland fisher lasses. Away out to sea congregations of long-tailed ducks were gathered and their soothing but rather sad cries of *Caloo-oo* were always associated in the minds of the islanders with fine weather. Along with those Caloo-oos were flocks of eider drakes. They left their wives to bring up the family and only returned when their young ones were old enough to fend for themselves. Perhaps because they had little to crow about, the eider drakes were very quiet except for an occasional soft 'quairk' like that of the domestic drake.

My village is now deserted by steam and sail and the herring fishing is no more. Some of the sounds I heard will never be heard again.

Oh my boatman Na hoire a aila
May joy await thee where e'er thou sailest,
When shall I see thee to-day, to-morrow?
Oh, do not leave me in lonely sorrow.

The Highland fisher lasses often sang these sad words. I can hear them still down through the years.

The Orcadian, September 10th 1959

DUEL ON THE FAIRWAY

R. T. JOHNSTON

(It is strange to think that that master of Orkney dialect and humour, Bob Johnston, came from Buckie, where his long career in journalism started with the Banffshire Advertiser. It was in July 1931 that he came to Orkney to take up a job as reporter on The Orkney Herald, a job to which he returned after wartime service. His self-effacing nature led him to use pen-names for his stories, two novels, and weekly cartoon feature by 'Spike'. Later, when he moved in the 1950s to The Press and Journal in Aberdeen, he wrote the 'Donovan Smith' column. In the mythical parish of Stenwick he distilled an Orkney which can often seem more real than today's changing scene, and his characters have taken a permanent place among the immortals.)

It is not generally known that there existed in Stenwick for a time, a golf club. It never really caught on to any great extent, and it is now defunct, the modest nine-hole course having returned to its natural state – from which, indeed, it had never very much departed – and having become once more over-run by real rabbits in place of the two-legged variety who occupied it during its brief heyday.

The club owed its inauguration to old Godfrey Ritch of Mucklegutter, as so many of Stenwick's institutions do. It was the outcome of a visit Godfrey had paid to a friend in St Andrews – not the East Mainland St Andrews, but the home of the Royal and Ancient game.

While he was there the friend had persuaded him to have a round of golf, and while the game itself did not greatly impress Godfrey, the subsequent session at the nineteenth hole roused him to the utmost enthusiasm. Tales are still told, I believe, of the bewhiskered Orkney veteran's carry-on in the august clubhouse. However that may be, Godfrey returned to Stenwick convinced that no Orkney parish should be without its golf clubhouse, and since one cannot very well have a clubhouse without having a club, he called a meeting of all interested and formed the Stenwick Golf Club. There were some twenty-five members, and the subscription was one guinea, the subscriptions being devoted to equipping the clubhouse with a bar, and those liquid commodities with which a bar is generally associated.

The club and the clubhouse functioned with great success for some two years, and then it was suggested by someone that the club ought to have a course, a suggestion which was put into force at the next annual general meeting.

There being few funds to spare on the construction of a really ambitious course, the course ultimately laid out was a somewhat rough and ready one, limited to nine holes which was, as Godfrey said, as much as anyone wanted to play at one time. The greens were small and there was little to distinguish them from the fairway, nor was there a great deal to distinguish the fairway from the rough. The course however, did not lack hazards. These it had in a profusion which would have made Henry Cotton or Bobby Locke take one look and withdraw, screaming, from the scene. The hazards included large clumps of stinging nettles, two extensive patches of bog (into one of which, it is said, Ronald Hourie vanished one night while playing a solitary round and was never seen again), four disused quarries, thirteen drystone dykes, a prehistoric earth dwelling (since taken over by the Office of Works), and an assortment of holes, ditches, cavities and what not.

This, however, is not a history of the Stenwick Golf Club, but rather the story of one particular match played during its existence.

Most of the club's membership was, naturally, male, but there was a small though active ladies' section, of which the leading lights were Mrs Boadicea Skea, the burly widow of Mucklebust, and Mrs Henrietta Kirkness, Godfrey Ritch's daughter, also a widow. Both these ladies took to golf like ducks to water, the more so, perhaps, as the male section of the club contained one or two eligible bachelors and widowers.

One of these bachelors, and by far the most eligible, was Bartholomew Spence of Sowfarrow, a robust, ruddy-faced individual with a liking for the ladies, but no liking for the halter of matrimony. Of all the members of the golf club, Bartholomew was the one who had been bitten most deeply by the insidious germ of the game. He became a golf fanatic. He assembled an array of clubs which, if placed end to end, would have stretched almost the length of the course, he would commandeer any discussion about fat stock prices and turn it into a saga of how he had done the tricky seventh hole in twelve, he could be seen flailing his way round the course at almost any hour between dawn and dusk, and he had presented three cups for competition by members of the club, all of which he had won himself with the greatest of ease.

Also, he had presented a cup for competition among the ladies' section, and it is upon this trophy that my story hangs. Four ladies, the full female membership, entered for the contest, namely Mrs Skea, Mrs Kirkness, Miss Janet Cutt (as she then was), the postmistress, and Mrs Delphine Budge of Snortquoy. Fate ordained that in the first round Mrs Skea should play Miss Cutt, and Mrs Kirkness Mrs Budge. Space does not allow me to go into detail about the games; suffice it to say that Boadicea thrashed Miss Cutt unmercifully, while Mrs Kirkness' victory over Mrs Budge was only a shade less emphatic.

Bartholomew Spence took the closest interest in the progress of the tournament, accompanying the players on their rounds and offering advice and criticism to every stroke played or missed. Probably this incessant babble on Spence's part had a good deal to do with the lamentable form displayed by Miss Cutt, an indifferent performer at the best of times and one who reacts badly to counsel, however wise and well-meant. For instance, when she swung ferociously on the first tee and sent the ball trickling only three inches, Bartholomew's comment of "Mighty, Chenet, if thoo hid gien doon ahint id on thee hands an' knees thoo could hiv blawn id further" was one which might have upset souls much less susceptible to criticism.

At all events Boadicea and Henrietta reached the final in the proverbial canter, and it was on the evening preceding the final that the incident occurred which gave the match its full atmosphere of drama.

Boadicea and Henrietta had been out on the course, independently of one another, getting themselves tuned up for the big contest, and on their return to the clubhouse they found there Bartholomew Spence, reclining in a cane chair, drinking home brewed ale, and boring three or four fellow members to tears with an account of how he had just missed doing the third hole in nine earlier in the evening.

"Weel," bawled Bartholomew, as Boadicea Skea lumbered in, "hoo wur thoo playin', Mrs Skea?"

"Oh middleen," said the large lady, but her glum look clearly indicated that she had found her form far from satisfactory.

"Middleen," echoed Spence. "Desh, Mrs Skea thoo'll hiv tae dae better than that tae win the cup. Wur thoo keepin' thee heid steady like I telt thee?"

"Yaas," said Boadicea.

"Weel whit wur wrang?"

"Oh noathing," said Mrs Skea. "I cheust wurno puttin' aafil weel."

At that moment the second of the finalists entered. She too wore a significantly tight-lipped expression.

"Ay Henrietta," Spence greeted her, "thoo dinno luk aafil plazed wi' theesel ither. Wur thoo aff thee game teu?"

Henrietta Kirkness brightened a little at his indication that Mrs Skea had been playing badly.

"I don't ken whit wur wrang wi' me," she said, "bit I cheust couldno hit the ball strite."

Bartholomew shook a disapproving head.

"That's no geud, Henrietta," he said. "Thoo kinno hit the ball aafil herd, bit thoo kin chenerally hit id strite. Desh, atween thee no hittin' the ball strite an' Boadicea no puttin' weel I kin see wur gaun tae hiv a final the morn that will no be worth a dochen."

"Weel weel," said Boadicea with a touch of irritation, "whit aboot id? Id's cheust a peedie cup wur playin' for, an' id's no muckle differ whar wins id."

"Cheust a peedie cup," cried Bartholomew, stung to the quick. "Desh, id's me trophy, an' id's up tae thee tae mak' a geud game o'd."

Henrietta glanced at him and shrugged.

"Mrs Skea's right," said she. "Id's cheust a peedie insignifeecant bit o' cup an' thir's no yeuse gettan all wund up aboot id. Id's no as if wae wur playin' for something worth."

Perhaps Bartholomew had been indulging in a little too much home brew. Perhaps this made him rash. At all events he now rose to his feet and burst out: "Weel wid thoo consider me worth tae play for?"

There was a silence. Everyone in the clubhouse stared at him, and none more intently than Boadicea Skea and Henrietta Kirkness.

"Whit dis thoo mean?" asked Mrs Kirkness.

"This is whit I mean," shouted Spence, hammering the top of the nearest table. "Id's weel kent that thoo an' Mrs Skea is been lukkin' for a man iver since thoo lost thee hussbands. Weel, a'll mairry the wen whar wins the cup next night. Whit dis thoo say tae yin?"

There was a long, throbbing silence, in which a handicap might have been heard to drop. Then Boadicea and Henrietta simultaneously drew a deep, deep breath, and looked at one another, and then back at Bartholomew.

"Thoo're no – thoo're no gockan iss?" inquired Mrs Skea, suspiciously.

"Not I," declared Spence. He rose solemnly to his feet, swayed a little, and drew his forefinger across his adam's apple. "Cut me throt," he stated. "A'll mairry the winner, whariver shae is, if I shid niver go fae here."

Henrietta Kirkness gulped. The thought that if she struck top form tomorrow night she would be rewarded with Bartholomew Spence and all his worldly goods almost made her imagination reel. Boadicea Skea felt the same. It was a moment large with destiny.

Henrietta snatched up the golfbag she had petulantly flung down on entering, and hurried out again, determination written large on her somewhat ferrety features. There was still sufficient light left for half an hour's golf and she meant to make the most of it. In a moment there came, from the direction of the first tee, the crack of a crisply-driven golfball.

"Yin soonded like a geud shot," commented Eustace Rosie.

Boadicea Skea was tired, but the idea of Henrietta Kirkness getting practice while she was not was more than she could bear. With a grunt she opened her locker, dragged out her clubs, and lumbered in the wake of her rival into the gathering twilight.

"Boy, Bartholomew," said Eustace Rosie, grinning, "thoo certainly gied them something tae fight for."

Spence rubbed his hands gleefully.

"Yaas, bit thoo're a right geup," observed Eustace tersely, rising and putting on his cap. "Still id's thee funeral."

In the ordinary way the final of the ladies' trophy would have aroused little interest, but the circumstances being what they were, some eighty to a hundred spectators turned up to watch the proceedings. Only a minority of the crowd were golfers, the rest being unable to tell the difference between a caddie and a mashie but considering that the spectacle of Boadicea and Henrietta battling for a husband was one likely to be fraught with interest.

Punctually at 7 o'clock the two contestants emerged from the clubhouse accompanied by Godfrey Ritch, who was to act as referee, and by Bartholomew Spence.

The gallery did not fail to note Bartholomew's expression, which was careworn in the extreme, for it was only now, when the exhilarating effects of last night's home brew had worn off, that realisation of the rash promise he had made had come home to Spence with sickening force.

As the two ladies made their way to the first tee he glanced furtively from one to the other, trying to make up his mind which would be the lesser of the two evils, but always coming to the same conclusion, that marriage to either would be a fate worse than death. He looked at the portentous Boadicea, clad, for the occasion, in a siren-suit that made her ample proportions look more ample than ever, and shuddered. He looked at Henrietta, scrawny and ferret-faced, and shuddered again. Then he looked at the sky, in the hope that Nature might intervene to save him with a typhoon, hurricane or earthquake, but there was nothing doing; Nature was in her most benign and placid mood. Bartholomew sighed deeply. It appeared as if his hours of happy bachelorhood were soon to be over.

"Weel lasses," said Godfrey crisply, producing a penny from his pocket, "thoo'll better toss for the honour o' drivin' aff. Heids or tells, Boadicea?"

"Heids," said the large lady, and heids it proved to be. Boadicea grunted with satisfaction, taking this as an omen for the outcome of the match, and prepared to drive off. The spectators gathered in an expectant semi-circle round the tee and there was some humorous comment as Mrs Skea bent wheezingly to place her ball in position.

"Tak' care thoo dinno split thee breeks Boadicea," observed Armstrong Tait, and indeed the nether portion of the massive widow's garment seemed to be taxed to the utmost to withstand the strain imposed on it.

Boadicea ignored the interruption, and straightening up with a puff, selected a driver, placed its head behind the ball, and stood motionless for a moment as if in prayer. Then she drew the club slowly back and swept it forward with terrific force.

The strong point about Boadicea's game was her driving, but too often as now, she was erratic. The ball screamed off the tee like a bullet, but at right angles to the direction of the green, and there was a wild shriek of pain from Galahad Davie as it hit him squarely on the temple, and rebounded seventy feet in the air to land about ten yards down the course.

Galahad crumpled moaning to the ground, and Boadicea directed a glare at his recumbent figure.

"Thoo deshed whalp," she boomed, "whit did thoo git in

me wey for? Yin ball wid hiv gien haff a mile."

The hapless Galahad being in no condition to reply, Boadicea vacated the tee with a snort, in favour of her opponent. Mrs Kirkness teed up with a thin smile.

Henrietta was a player of quite a different stamp from Boadicea. The latter depended on hitting power and the assistance of Providence to see that her hits went where they were intended to; the former relied on a policy of caution, and the avoidance of any shot, however spectacular, which might get distance at the expense of accuracy. Her drive from the first tee was typical of her approach to the game. Holding her club at the middle of the shaft and limiting her back swing to four inches, she gave the ball a sharp rap which sent it bouncing greatly down the fairway for a distance of about 20 yards in a dead straight line. Well satisfied with this performance, she shouldered her bag and marched off on its trail.

Boadicea took a brassie for her second stroke, and putting every ounce of her 22 stone into her swing, hit what is known in golfing circles as a screamer, straight as a die. The only trouble was that the ball did not touch down until it was some 150 yards past the green. Mrs Kirkness, for her part, took a full iron and advanced a good fifteen yards. She was on the green with her tenth stroke. Something that looked like a volcanic eruption on the skyline told where Boadicea was still manfully trying to get out of the small quarry into which she had landed with her fourth. Henrietta sank a two inch putt to get down in fifteen, and Boadicea, still in the quarry, conceded the hole.

"Boy," said Eustace Rosie to Bartholomew Spence as the players proceeded to the second tee, "whar dis thoo think will win?"

Spence uttered a morose grunt. He did not care a docken who won. The only thing certain was that, whoever won, he, Bartholomew Spence would be the loser.

"I think mesel that Henrietta will win," proceeded Eustace. "Shae's aafil steady. Boadicea is ower rammish. Thoo niver ken whar shae'll pit the ball. Yaas boy, id luks as if Godfrey

Ritch will be thee fether-in-laa in a peedie while."

"Geud goad," exclaimed Bartholomew, paling. This had not occurred to him.

Mrs Kirkness was smiling confidently as she achieved a decorous ten-yarder from the second tee. It seemed to her that all she had to do was play her normal steady game and she would win in a canter while her opponent rampaged all over the countryside. Indeed Henrietta had visions of the game ending at the fifth green, and she was already planning her trousseau when Boadicea stepped up to drive.

The widow of Mucklebust's face was grim. Henrietta's success at the first hole had put her on her mettle, and she was filled with a passionate desire to "wipe the smirk aff yin peedie whalp's fiss," as she inwardly phrased it. Unfortunately one of the weaknesses of Mrs Skea's golf was that she was incapable of learning from her mistakes. She had sliced at the first hole; she now sliced again, and this time there was no convenient Galahad Davie to intercept, and the ball screamed off in the general direction of the Brough of Birsay, to alight ultimately in the boggiest patch of bog in the West Mainland and vanish from human ken. Henrietta won the hole comfortably, and with Boadicea's driving going from bad to worse, she went on to win the third and fourth as well, despite taking eight putts on the fourth green.

Gloom settled on Boadicea's supporters. "Hid's all ower ber the shouteen," said Willie Budge of Snortquoy to his wife. "Henrietta Kirkness cheust needs tae win wen more hole. Desh that teu, for I wid ferly like tae hiv seen Boadicea gittan Spence for a hussband."

Willie's opinion was generally shared, yet such was the fascination of the match that no-one thought of leaving.

Eustace Rosie nudged Bartholomew Spence.

"Weel boy," he said, "id luks as if Mrs Kirkness will be thee bride. Shae's wackin' awey wi' the match. Are thoo plazed?"

If Bartholomew was pleased he concealed the fact admirably. While Henrietta had been piling up her lead his sympathies had been turning more and more to Boadicea.

She was no more desirable to him as a wife than she had ever been, but at least he felt that her golf had more dash and spirit about it than the miserable tip-tapping of Mrs Kirkness. Viewing the two contestants merely as golfing partners and not as bedmates he felt that he would infinitely rather play with Boadicea than with Henrietta. Boadicea's golf might exasperate him, but Henrietta's would drive him insane.

It is well said that golf is an uncertain game. Hitherto in the match the Imp of Fortune had remained sneeringly aloof from Boadicea. Now, at the fifth tee, no doubt conscience-stricken, he rushed to her aid.

Henrietta having made her customary jab thirty feet or so down the fairway, Boadicea stepped to the tee, broodingly snatched out the nearest club in her bag – a putter – and hit the drive of a lifetime, a low, whistling shot, straight as a die, which laid the ball on the green eighteen inches from the pin.

"My mighty," gasped the large lady. "Yin wur a deeker."

Henrietta Kirkness compressed her lips. After that shot it would take some doing for her to win this hole, even admitting the unlikely possibility that Boadicea would take four or five putts. She deserted her usual cautious methods and aimed a mighty swing at her ball, only to miss it completely and fall flat on her face in a clump of nettles.

Rising she said, through gritted teeth: "Hid's thee hole, Mrs Skea."

Boadicea drove from the sixth tee with fresh hope animating her expansive bosom. It was a powerful drive, but badly pulled. However, the ball struck the top of a dyke, zoomed back into the straight, hit a grazing ewe, and zig-zagged sportively on to the green.

There was a click as Mrs Kirkness's jaw dropped.

"The luck o' some fock," she exclaimed in a quivering voice.

"Come wi' less o'd, Henrietta Kirkness," snapped Mrs Skea. "Play thee shot an' no so muckle yap."

Fuming Mrs Kirkness drove. The ball rolled sedately a dozen feet and disappeared down a rabbit hole. Boadicea marched to the green, swung her putter, and sank a twelve-foot putt with the utmost nonchalance.

Henrietta debated for a moment the likelihood that she would cover 200 yards in one hit, decided that it was beyond her and conceded the hole with an ill grace.

"Boy," said Ambrose Wylie to Peedie Tam of Quoydunt, "the game's' no ower yet. Mrs Skea is makkin' a come-back."

And Bartholomew Spence, watching the game with the same fascination as a condemned felon is said to watch the erection of the gallows, realised that the identity of his bride-to-be was still anybody's guess.

Boadicea's success had caused her to swing from blackest gloom to buoyant confidence. Correspondingly Mrs Kirkness was badly rattled. She breathed a little more easily when she saw Mrs Skea's drive from the seventh take off like a Vampire jet and disappear into a wilderness of bracken 80 or 90 yards beyond the green, but in her own eagerness to get a little more distance than usual she topped her drive badly and succeeded only in dislodging the ball from its tee.

"Desh that noo," she exclaimed in vexation. Old Godfrey, who, with a fine disregard for the duties of a referee, had spent most of the game in the clubhouse imbibing home brew and had only been lured back to the course by the news that a tight finish was in prospect, gave his daughter a severe poke in the ribs.

"Henrietta," he declared, "thoo're playin' like a clurt. Pull theesel thegither or thoo'll loss the game, an' a'll loss the chance o' gettan thee aff me hends at last."

Boadicea stumped off on the long trek in search of her ball, and found it in a position which might have daunted the heart of a Dai Rees, deeply embedded in tough bracken roots. Undismayed, she carved at it with her niblick till it finally shot out of its lodgment in a spray of leaves and small twigs and came to earth within chipping distance of the green.

Henrietta's snail-like progress down the straight took her to the green in nine and she smiled for the first time for half an hour, for she saw that she was well-placed to win the hole and the match, for Boadicea's flailings in the rough had cost eight strokes.

Once again, however, Henrietta failed to allow for the unexpected. Just as she turned to select her putter something struck her a sharp blow on the base of the skull, and the next thing she knew was having water sprinkled on her face by a sympathetic spectator.

"Whit happened?" she gasped.

"Thoo'll niver guess," was the reply. "Boadicea played her shot an' the ball hat thee on the back o' the heid an' darted back an' gied right in the hole."

Henrietta felt a sense of despair. How could anyone compete against such phenomenal luck? she asked her father.

The veteran pulled his whiskers. "Best kens," he admitted frankly, "bit id kinno lest. Cheust thoo play thee yeusual an' thoo'll win yet."

The advice was good, but Henrietta, what with the knock on the head and shattered confidence, was incapable of playing her usual. At the eighth she had the mortification of slicing her ball into the sand-box and taking fourteen strokes to extricate it, while Mrs Skea got down in 20 to win the hole and square the match.

Armstrong Tait threw his cap in the air and shouted, "Geud for thee Boadicea, thoo're gaun tae win. Keep id up.' And Bartholomew Spence realised with a shock that Boadicea, and not Henrietta, now looked like becoming his life partner. Boadicea, in fact, turned and gave him a gaze of proud ownership which curdled his blood.

It is strange thing that while Mrs Kirkness had appeared to be heading for victory Spence had felt Mrs Skea to be slightly the more desirable – or at least slightly the less undesirable – of the two, but now that Mrs Skea was staging a grandstand finish and Henrietta appeared to have shot her bolt, he found himself inclining to a preference for Mrs Kirkness. He told himself that at least Henrietta would be a wife he could boss around, while any attempt to boss Boadicea would simply be asking for an almighty cloor on the side of the head.

Weel weel, he thought despondently, the next hole would decide his fate. Although it was a warm night a cold sweat covered his forehead, his knees felt weak, and there was a sick emptiness at the pit of his stomach.

When Eustace Rosie clapped him genially on the shoulder and exclaimed: "Hid'll no be lang noo, boy,' he snarled: "Ah stoop, for goad's seck, thoo yap o' dirt, thoo're niver deun yappin'."

"Oh, is that so?" snorted Eustace indignantly, "Weel onywey a'm niver yapped mesel intae the fix that thoo're in this night. I hopp the match is a draa an' then thoo'll hiv tae mairry the two o' them."

With that Eustace stalked off in high dudgeon.

Meanwhile old Godfrey Ritch was trying to calm his daughter, who was having a mild form of hysterics.

"Tak' id aisy lass," he counselled, "an' stop boglin'. Mrs Skea kinno hae the luck all the time."

"That's whit thoo said afore," wailed Henrietta, "bit shae's still haein' id."

"Weel, feth, shae's no hivvin' id noo," said Godfrey, for Mrs Skea had just driven off, executing a disastrous pull which landed her ball in a ruined croft some 200 yards to the left of the tee. Moreover, so vigorous had been her follow-through that she had cracked herself on the back of the knee with the club-head, and was hopping ponderously about the tee, bawling with pain.

"There noo," said Godfrey gleefully to his daughter. "Noo's thee chance. Shae'll niver git oot o' yin croft, an' shae's crippled hersel as weel. Play thee yeusual game an' Bartholomew Spence is thine."

Henrietta smiled through her tears, and with a hypocritical, "Thoo're no hurt theesel Boadicea, I hopp," she shoved the large lady out of the way, teed up and played a safe thirteen-yarder down the middle.

An enthralled crowd followed Boadicea as she hobbled to the ruined croft behind whose roofless walls her ball lurked coyly. Most of the spectators shared Godfrey's opinion that the ruin constituted a hazard from with the burly widow would be unable to extricate herself, but these reckoned without Mrs Skea's resource.

Squeezing her great bulk through the doorway of the croft, she leaned against the wall from inside and heaved. The wall quivered, swayed, and collapsed in a pile of dusty rubble, and Mrs Skea, with a clear view to the fairway, took her niblick and whacked the ball well and truly back to the course.

A thunderstruck Henrietta Kirkness saw the little white sphere drop out of the blue and bound on to the green. She turned an anguished face on her sire.

"Did thoo see yin?" she screamed. "A'm feenished."

"No thoo're no," snapped Godfrey. He pulled fiercely at his whiskers. "A'm the referee, an' I hiv something tae say. Hey Mrs Skea," he roared, "Come here."

Boadicea, followed by her swarm of admirers, limped up inquiringly.

"Weel," she asked, "whit is id? Is thee dowter concedin' the match?"

"Not shae," said old Ritch. "Shae's the winner."

Boadicea looked blank. "Whit wey that?"

"Thoo're disqualeefied," said Godfrey amiably.

Boadicea's eyes narrowed, and her teeth met with a click. "Disqualeefied?" she rumbled. "Whit for? Whit am I deun?"

"Thoo interfered wi' the hazards," said Godfrey. "Thoo shoved doon the wall o' yin croft the wey thoo wid can tae play oot. Whar wid golf be if players wis tae knock doon the obstacles o' the corse?"

"Desh thee," howled the large lady, "yin croft is no even on the corse."

"Thoo wur in id," retorted Godfrey, "so id's bound tae be."

There were angry shouts from Boadicea's fans. "Play the game, Godfrey Ritch," cried Inigo Pottinger, and Armstrong Tait shouted: "Thoo deshed ould chitt, thoo cheust want thee own dowter tae win."

"A'm gaun tae play on," declared Boadicea.

"Thoo kinno," said Godfrey. "A'm telt thee, thoo're

disqualeefied. Henrietta Kirkness wins the match."

These were almost the last words he ever uttered. Boadicea was still clutching her niblick in her hand. With a deep-toned howl of rage she whirled it round her head and lashed at the veteran. Only a quick backward leap saved Godfrey from decapitation; as it was, the blade of the niblick swished through his whiskers, grazing his chin. Before Mrs Skea could launch another swing he had turned and was galloping towards the clubhouse with an agility incredible in one of his age. Boadicea, brandishing her niblick and waking the echoes with her wrathful bellowing, gave chase, but handicapped by her sore knee it was obvious that she had little hope of overtaking the sprightly veteran.

And what of the victorious Henrietta? Beaming with happiness she was scurrying in and out of the crowd, crying "Bartholomew, whar are thee? Come here boy, an' gie thee peedie bride-tae-be a kess."

But answer there was none. Bartholomew was not among those present, and Eustace Rosie said that now he came to think of it he had not seen Bartholomew since the eighth green. A hue and cry was raised. The course was searched from end to end, but no Bartholomew.

Enlightenment came when the searchers returned to the clubhouse. There was a note there from Bartholomew. He extended his apologies to the winner of the match, but he had come to the conclusion that he could not see his way to getting married after all. He was, he added, leaving Stenwick for an indefinite period, and would no doubt return when all had been forgiven and forgotten. In conclusion he congratulated whoever had won the match, and hoped she would treasure the trophy.

One regrets to say that Henrietta placed the Ladies Cup on the clubhouse floor and hammered it into a shapeless mass with the head of her mashie.

Orcadian Nights

MEMORIES OF JO GRIMOND

HOWIE FIRTH

(This was broadcast on the news of Lord Grimond's death.)

To a whole generation of us, Jo Grimond was as integral a part of Orkney as Skara Brae or St Magnus Cathedral. He became a national figure by sheer flair, with the kind of natural elegance that you only find in the true masters of their field. It's the assurance of the cricketer who stands at the crease and casually flicks the fast bowler to the boundary. In the north, where the winters are long and dark and made for reading books, intellectual skill is prized, and in conciseness of thought and clearness of vision, Jo Grimond shone.

I remember recording a radio interview with him in the 1987 election, when he was well into retirement, but clearly delighted to have an opportunity to float ideas. Did he think, I asked him, that the Tories under Mrs Thatcher had become the new radicals? His reply, sparkling and incisive, would grace any political manifesto of the present time.

When I stood against him in the 1974 general election, I didn't realise at the time how it would produce a kind of bond. Jo had the professional's eye in politics, and anyone who had become involved had joined the club – particularly if they were there to share ideas. Interviewing him subsequently for radio became something like turning the pages of a friend's photograph album. He would talk about the great political hecklers of Orkney and Shetland, from the days before television when political meetings were glorious confrontations of marvellous repartee; he would recall the epic journeys around the constituency in election campaigns where every island must be visited, by small boat or aeroplane. In the early days after the war, the candidates had often to travel around together on the steamer, and would land at various island piers to speak to the assembled populace, one by one.

One of Jo's strongest Orkney supporters was a man who divided the world into two categories – Tories, who were 'rank'; and Liberals, who were 'staunch.' Jo as a man, and as representative of the party which when in government had brought in the crofting legislation, inspired such support. And he was a staunch friend of the isles; as one of his lifelong Shetland friends well put it, when the chips were down, you knew you could rely on him. In the late sixties, for example, he fought tirelessly, courageously and articulately to keep the island authorities of Orkney and Shetland from absorption into the new super-regions of mainland Scotland. In the seventies, he steered through Parliament the legislation that gave Orkney and Shetland unique powers to control oil development for community benefit. I can remember the former Shetland Chief Executive, Ian Clark, describing the skill with which Jo would take from him highly complex and detailed documents, often with only a matter of minutes left before facing a Commons Committee, and identify the key points to highlight or beware.

He was all too unusual in a politician because he had a long-term vision that covered all of society, combined with a warm humour and immense personal charm. He looked like a leader, in a way like an aristocrat from another age, and yet he appealed to the ordinary person because he spoke not with slogans, but with logic and clarity. He respected his audience's intellect, and invited them to join him in his analysis of political ideas. It was appropriate that someone who looked so much like a Prime Minister should marry the grand-daughter of Mr Asquith, and a brilliant political thinker and activist in her own right. In his talents, Jo Grimond harked back to a past age of greatness, but in his thinking he charted a course for the future. It really is this evening as if a light has gone out in the north, and a time for many memories.

BBC Radio Scotland, October 25th 1993

ENTERING PARLIAMENT

JO GRIMOND

(Amongst Jo Grimond's many talents was writing; he was as naturally fluent with a pen as on a public platform, as his Memoirs, published in 1979, showed.)

I nearly did not fight the 1950 Election. The outlook for Liberals was bleak. I was due to go to work for Collins, the publishers. In preparation for this I put in a few weeks with a printer in Edinburgh. Ever since then I have sympathised with the anarchism which machine-minding engenders. After an hour I was bored to distraction. I went to the lavatory as often as possible. I was tempted to throw spanners in the works. Talk about clock-watching: I looked at my watch every ten minutes.

Now I am very glad I did fight the election. The opposition was strong. Sir Basil Neven-Spence, the sitting Member, was a Shetlander, well-liked and deservedly so. He was rejected for no better reason than the electors thought he had been in Parliament long enough. The Labour candidate was Harald Leslie, the Assistant Adjutant General of my war-time experience, an Orcadian devoted to his home islands, with a delightful Orcadian wife who had been the doctor on an Orkney island. For any other Party he would certainly have got in for Orkney and Shetland and as a Labour candidate for many other Scottish constituencies, but he wanted to be MP for his native islands and they were not inclined to his Party.

The election meetings in 1950 were the most crowded I can remember. Not that any were large, but four times a night I would find several rows of black-suited and black-capped crofters waiting in the halls or schools. They sat patiently, often in desks designed for the infant class – like large birds on small nests. There were no air services round the islands in those days nor vehicle ferries between them. In Shetland candidates went to Yell and Unst either in launches or in the *Earl of Zetland*. The *Earl* was a comfortable enough ship but in rough weather she bobbed about like a cork. She is the only vessel plying around Orkney and Shetland on which I have been sick (and that only once). I was sick on a fishing boat but that was due to an unwise tea of fish livers in the hot and diesel-fume laden cabin.

During the '50 Election which was held in March the weather was rough. Sir Basil was out of action for twenty-four hours while the *Earl* was hove-to behind an island for shelter. To smaller islands the voyage had to be made in hired boats. We were once accompanied by a killer whale, no doubt with hope that we would capsize – but he (or she) was disappointed. There were few piers at which the *Earl* could tie up. Passengers, cattle, sheep, crates and numerous cargo of all kinds were ferried ashore in undecked 'flit' boats, cumbersome affairs in which you could get very wet.

For an evening meeting you had to spend the night on the island. As there were some twenty parishes each on the mainlands of Orkney and Shetland, in addition to the outlying islands, the programme was pretty heavy. I addressed over a hundred meetings. In Orkney the northern outlying islands were served by two small steamers, the *Earl Thorfinn* and the *Earl Sigurd*. They took all day to get round. At times this was inconvenient but many farmers enjoyed the trip. At each pier they had time to chat to their friends and even take a cup of tea. The South Isles of Orkney were served by two old naval drifters. The skippers grew old along with their boats. I was travelling in the wheelhouse one day when the skipper let out a piercing shriek down the speaking tube. 'The engineer's a bit deaf,' he explained. 'When he hears that he knows it's time to stop.' Speaking of the companion ship, he announced, I thought, 'that she was *done*.' When I said that she didn't seem to do too badly, 'It's not the ship,' he explained with disdain, 'It's the skipper, his legs are done.'

The islanders of North Ronaldsay voted on the neighbouring island of Sanday. The custom, illegal I suspect, was that the candidates clubbed together to charter a boat to take them to the polls. Sanday had a pub: North Ronaldsay did not. It was probable that many of the visitors did not vote. North Ronaldsay had, and has, another peculiarity. The sheep except at lambing time are kept outside a dyke which runs round the shore just above the water mark. They feed on seaweed and marram grass. Like the Shetland sheep to whom they must be related, by life-style if not by parentage, they have grown athletic. They can be seen leaping about the rocks like chamois.

As one might expect, the essence of Orkney and Shetland is distilled in the outlying islands. They are free, or were free, even from the urban taint of Kirkwall and Lerwick. In the island of Sanday in Orkney the Chair was taken by the schoolmaster, Mr Mackay. Mr Mackay was a man who never exposed how he voted. However, he was a glutton for political discussion. He had lived all his life in the North Isles, having been born on the little island of Papa Westray. All his life he had bought books. They cascaded from cupboards and stood in stacks around the furniture. Before the meeting it was customary to partake of a high tea provided by his admirable housekeeper. During this meal Mr Mackay discoursed and questioned upon literature, politics, Orkney and education. In Skerries, which are two rocky islets to the east of Shetland, the schoolmaster used to drive every available inhabitant to the meeting (there were only a hundred all told). All the dogs and babies had therefore to come too. They sat round the hall like one of those Victorian paintings – say by Sir David Wilkie.

I never canvassed. To ask anyone how they were going to vote would have seemed impudent to many of my constituents. Laura once approached the subject obliquely by asking a man how he thought his Papa Westray parish would vote. She got a terse and dusty answer. 'The folk in this parish will vote as they think fit. They will vote Liberal if they be of that mind.' If you called at a house you were expected to stay for a cup of tea or a 'refreshment.' To bang on a knocker, thrust a pamphlet and run away would have been considered rude. So most electioneering was done at meetings, sometimes, if time was short, a meeting at the pier, speaking from a barrel while loading or unloading proceeded.

There were, as I have said, four local weekly papers, two in Orkney, two in Shetland. They were violently partisan, two Liberal, two Tory. Indeed, the last issues before polling day of the Orkney papers were largely given over to propaganda and abuse of the other parties. This has gradually died out as our papers have been reduced to two and the Labour Party and SNP have to be accommodated. Also, I fear, apathy and television have smothered local enthusiasm. But the standard and leadership of the local papers under Gerry Meyer and Basil Wishart remains very high. I was much helped by Basil Wishart's brilliant journalism in Shetland, particularly in the lay-out of my election addresses, and by the Twatt family, owners and editors of the *Orkney Herald*.

When the poll was declared on Monday, 27th February 1950 (polling day having been the previous Thursday – so long did it take the boats to bring in the boxes from the outlying islands) I could hardly believe that I had been elected. I had long wanted to be an MP: for a Liberal that was in itself a remote possibility: now I was not only an MP but MP for Orkney and Shetland which to me was the most romantic of all constituencies. After the declaration of the poll I drove round Orkney, coming down the road into Stenness from the Orphir hills, seeing the lochs lying all peaceful in the fading light and thinking that even if it was only for a few months it was well worth it. By that time it was known that Labour would have a small majority. The *News Chronicle* doubted whether a government could survive with a majority of eight or ten. Even then, though, I was under no illusion that I had done it all myself. Laura deserved most credit at that election as at subsequent ones: Laura and such supporters as Edwin Eunson, the Tullochs, Charles Tait, Basil Wishart, the Twatts and the contributors to *Liberal Orkney*, a paper which Ernest Marwick and others produced during elections. It was significant that in the 1970 Election when Laura was away I did not do so well, being saved from doing much worse by Grizelda. My children and others were particularly good at designing posters which were a feature of elections in the fifties and sixties. 'Vote for Grimond – disregard the ex-Spence'; one Tory poster simply said 'Don't fiddle – Ban-Jo.' Jackie Robertson, who was my Agent for so long, thought of 'Vote for Jo – the man you know' – which adorned many an Orkney gatepost.

Memoirs (1979)

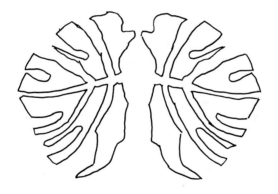

LAURA GRIMOND

HOWIE FIRTH

(This is the text given in St Magnus Cathedral on the occasion of the funeral of Lady Grimond.)

Laura Grimond came from one of the most outstanding political families in the British Isles. Her grandfather was Henry Herbert Asquith, Prime Minister from 1908 to 1916 in a great reforming government whose benefits continue into the present day.

She grew up in a household which sparkled with ideas and intellect. Her father, Sir Maurice Bonham Carter, had been Asquith's private secretary; her mother, Lady Violet, was Asquith's daughter, and the young Bonham Carters were able to spend Christmases and other times of the year with their grandfather himself. He used to treat them as adults, and the discussions often included the common bond of a love of books.

The children's education was broad and varied, under the teaching of several governesses, which left additional time for more reading and subsequently travel. Laura spent time in Vienna and Paris before her coming-out season as a debutante.

She was very beautiful, and immensely full of life, and the photographs in the family album include one of her climbing a high tree, and another of her playing leapfrog and jumping high in the air over Mr Asquith's second wife, Margot. It must have been quite clear that the man who was going to marry her would have to have a brilliance and a style of his own, and the young Jo Grimond had all of that. There was a slight pause while Lady Violet wondered whether Jo's prospects in the world should be carefully weighed up, and Sir Maurice was deputed to take him aside for a discussion on the subject. Fortunately, however, Sir Maurice kept the conversation entirely to other matters, and Jo and Laura were married in 1938.

Jo Grimond found his whole family of in-laws fascinating for their sheer glorious vitality and style. They had, he observed, 'a streak of true Asquithian colour,' with mental sinew, intellect and above all a tremendous characteristic of total loyalty, which became even stronger when the going got tough. Laura soon had to show her resourcefulness, when the War took Jo away to the army and she had to leave London and live in various parts of the country. She was just out of her teens and between short visits together she had to cope with wartime conditions, look after members of their families, and then bring up their own children.

She was a natural writer, and her letters to Jo were full of detail and incident and above all vitality and humour. A wonderful humour that overarched everything else with a kind of dashing panache was a family characteristic. It was a part of a joy in life but also of a resilience that strengthened them in time of adversity. That resilience and humour was to be drawn on even further when Jo's future turned towards politics, and Orkney and Shetland in the 1945 election.

Jo did not expect to win, but Orkney and Shetland warmed to him to the extent that he was less than four hundred votes short of victory, and so the long haul then began to make sure of the 1950 election, which took him into Parliament.

The work to cover the constituency, both in those election campaigns and throughout his subsequent career in Westminster, was immense, and one of the keys to victory was the work carried out by Laura. She knew that success depended on detail, on planning election itineraries, on fundraising, on organisation and timing, and with the family characteristic of total loyalty and commitment, she put her energies into building from the base upwards, and whatever the task, she led by example.

In those election campaigns, each island had to be visited, by steamer or small boat, and there was a sense of adventure about a campaign which involved Foula and Fair Isle and Papa Stour. There were parts of the constituency where virtually the whole population would turn out to hear all the candidates, and there were other areas where only one person ever went along, to grill each candidate in detail and then faithfully report back the verdict to the rest of the community. Everywhere had to be visited. Jo's rapid advance in national politics meant that Laura had increasingly to speak in her own right, and her clarity of thought and sheer lucidity of argument showed that she had inherited all the political flair of her family.

It was characteristic of her that what was memorable about it all to her was not the sheer amount of time and energy that she gave: instead she savoured the opportunity that she had to enjoy people and events. It was a time when elections in Orkney and Shetland were fought with great colour and style. There were supporters like the man in Finstown who was wont to divide the world into two categories, the Liberals, who were 'staunch,' and the Tories, who were 'rank.' There were hecklers whose remarks became the stuff of legend, to be joyously retold to family and friends.

The delight in humour was part of the great bond that ran so deep between Laura and Orkney and Shetland. Her family traditions of brilliant wit found a kindred community where stories of characters and worthies were savoured and where even the greyest and wettest winter's day could be lit up by a gem of a remark. A gleam would come into her eye, and the start of a laugh, and you could suddenly see the enchantment that had been there all her life and which some people makes them never seem to grow old.

She had a wonderfully elegant way of summing things up, and putting them in perspective. 'All piers,' she told an appreciative audience on sea transport in Kirkwall in March 1969, 'come in three sorts. There are some that go too far into the sea, some that go too far out of the sea, and some that never reach the sea at all.' She prefaced the discussion by telling the audience that she approached the subject of piers with considerable hesitation, as in her experience they were places were angels feared to tread. At the beginning, no one could be brought to agree on where they should be sited. And once they had been begun nobody could predict or knew where they were going to end.

She had a very deep feeling for landscape and buildings, which never left her. It combined the eye of the artist with the belief that people deserved to live in pleasant surroundings. Leading again by example, she put immense energy and effort into a series of successful conservation projects. There was the establishment of the Hoy Trust, and the purchase and restoration of the Strynd houses. Without her, Papdale House would have become bottoming for the modern school hostel, and the now highly useful old Stromness Academy building would be no more.

Laura's campaigns were always fought with tenacity and flair, as a general would hold the line and skilfully deploy his troops. The fight to save Papdale House looked about as uphill a struggle as you could get, but she brought in Magnus Magnusson and Maurice Lindsay and the poet Sir John Betjeman, whose feelings for the beauty of old architecture and the barbarities of the new equalled her own. He arrived in Orkney on a day described by Jo as 'one of those dreich days when the sky seems to be on the roof and every bush is shrivelled with wind, salt and rain – days known in Orkney as *coorse*.' Sir John was, however, utterly undaunted by the weather and utterly entranced by the view, and his readings of his own poetry at the concert in aid of the newly-formed Orkney Heritage Society were spell-binding.

In all this work, Laura was looking not just at the past for its own sake, but at enabling a future generation to enjoy it. The Hoy Trust, she emphasised, was there to preserve the magnificent scenery of the area, certainly, but it was first and foremost for the people who lived there. And the greatest cause of all was simply other people, taking up the case of those with problems, visiting those who were ill or handicapped or with someone to look after, finding time to introduce someone to others of kindred interest, writing to encourage someone through a time of difficulty, putting in a word for someone who needed help. She helped as an individual, and she helped as an MP's wife, and she helped through serving as an office-bearer for numerous organisations like the Guides and Women's Guild and many, many more. She served with distinction for six years as Orkney Islands Councillor for Firth and Harray, during which time she chaired the Social Work and Housing Committee with ability and compassion.

In her determination to help others through the world and put their welfare above her own, she was rather like one of the noblest and finest characters in Scottish literature, the schoolmaster in James Bridie's play 'Mr Gillie': what happened to one's self was utterly unimportant – the real satisfaction in life was helping others to bring out the best in themselves.

Latterly her illness limited her efforts towards the various causes she had worked so hard for. She heard the good news of progress on St Boniface Church in Papay but knew that there were more buildings to be saved; she saw the Orkney Mental Health Association building up from the solid foundation she had put so much work into laying, but knew how much needed to be done to help so many carers; and having so often run a stall for the 'Save the Children' Fund at the St Magnus Fair and the County Show, she shared the deep anguish of many people at the suffering of the people of Bosnia and the all too limited assistance from the western world so far. She would, I am sure, be quite embarrassed that people were gathered together here to listen to an account of her own life and much rather want everyone to think instead about the work of these various organisations for whom today's collection will be given.

She died on February 15th, exactly 66 years after her grandfather, the Earl of Oxford and Asquith, and the epitaph written for him by a newspaper editor of the day would apply to her just as accurately. 'No man who ever played a great part in affairs was more conspicuously free from the common vices of public life... His loyalty to his colleagues was one of his most striking attributes... He will live in history as a type of all that is best in the English character.' To which we would add – and the Orcadian character as well. She will be missed very much, but she leaves behind an enormous amount of good that many, many others will benefit from for a very, very long time.

St Magnus Cathedral, February 21st 1994

SOME ORKNEY ARTISTS

JO GRIMOND

When we first settled in Orkney the local chief magistrate, the Sheriff (or Sheriff-Substitute as he was then called) was Barrigal Keith. The Keiths were, like the Playfairs and Boases of St Andrews, a family of distinction. One of Barrigal's cousins, Berriedale Keith, wrote a text book on constitutional law while Professor of Sanskrit at Edinburgh University. The Keiths came from Thurso across the Pentland Firth where Barrigal had a collection of modern Scottish pictures by artists such as Peploe, Leslie Hunter, Cadell and Gillies.

Sheriff Keith not only collected pictures but painted himself. He could be seen, looking like Sir Walter Scott, painting in Kirkwall and like many artists rather tetchy if interrupted. He and the art teachers were partly responsible for the surge in painting which has swept Orkney and to some extent Shetland since the war. Ian MacInnes now the Rector of Stromness Academy, Nancy Hewison and Sylvia Wishart are only a few of the painters whose pictures give a better impression of Orkney, its landscapes, its sea-scapes and the streets of Stromness and Kirkwall than anything I can write.

I say 'partly responsible' because the urge to paint, carve, work in wood is endemic in Orkney and Shetland. Many cottages have pictures of ships in which local people sailed. Orkney chairs with their high straw backs are still hand-made. In the remote island of North Ronaldsay the Scotts, particularly the sculptor, Ian Scott, have a hereditary eye for shape and atmosphere. I have two small sculptures of otters and porpoises carved from local stone by John Williamson of Lubba in Shetland which catch the grace of these animals while escaping the slickness of popular models. Both Mr Rae in Shetland and

Miss Ola Gorie in Orkney have revived traditional designs in silver jewellery while in Mr Robert Rendall, a draper to trade, we had a poet and conchologist of more than local fame. Mr Rendall when I knew him was almost stone deaf but whenever he came to London I would get him tickets for the gallery of the House of Commons. The faces of MPs fascinated him, why I was never quite sure.

But the patriarch of Orkney art, though not in the least elderly either in manner or vision, was Stanley Cursiter. Stanley had been keeper of the National Gallery of Scotland and though subject to rheumatism was still painting when we came to Orkney. For shelter from the gales he had a contraption like a mobile greenhouse. At first I did not take so much to his paintings as to himself but that was because I first saw his more formal set-pieces, some of them done as the Queen's Limner. Later I grew to like his Orkney pictures very much indeed.

By the late sixties he was nearly eighty, confined for most of the time to his house in Stromness which he had re-modelled and decorated. There we would visit him in the gable-end which stood with its feet in the harbour as he sat dispensing sherry, feeding his tame sea-gull and looking down Scapa Flow with the hills of Hoy on one side and the greens and yellows of Orphir on the other. The sea-gull was a combative bird which showed the scars of the fights in which as it grew older it was not always victorious. Stanley was of the stamp of Edwin Muir, reflective, enthusiastic, spry, with bright eyes below white eyebrows, devoted to Orkney and always keen to discuss her future.

He was I am sure a trial to his tailor (a phrase of his own) for he was always impeccably dressed. He was fastidious in whatever he did. His prose, like his painting, was concise, though both could have a lyrical quality. He wrote a book about himself in seventy pages and a life of Peploe from which I have gathered more knowledge and feeling about art than from anything else except Patrick Heron's talk. His *Peploe* is almost as slim as his autobiography, but both give the heart and spine of the matters in hand. Everyone who has ever tried knows how difficult it is to end a book. *Peploe* has a perfect finish. 'These pages are but a gesture – a hand waved in greeting and farewell.'

As I am myself chronically disorganised, my room loaded with pictures, papers, books, furniture, I particularly admire those who are orderly, especially when they have a touch of genius as well. High in this galère I put Stanley Cursiter, along with my father, Moira Kennedy and Jasper Ridley. Laura was inspired to get Ian Scott, the North Ronaldsay sculptor, to carve a bust of Stanley which now stands with those of Edwin Muir and Eric Linklater in the County Library commemorating three Orcadians who were friends and companions in the Arts.

John Betjeman was much taken with the north and occasionally stayed with us. He was a most heart-warming guest. On arriving at the Old Manse on one of those dreich days when the sky seems to be on the roof and every bush is shrivelled with wind, salt and rain – days known in Orkney as 'coarse' – he fell into an ecstasy over Jimmy Brown's haystacks investing them with a Monet-like beauty which up till then we had not appreciated. He also managed to convey to Laura the impression that she had personally sited them outside the window especially for his pleasure.

Stanley Cursiter and John Betjeman got on like houses on fire. A largely illegible letter from John describes a visit to Stanley's Stromness house where he saw 'Two exquisite Brabazonish water-colours by him (Cursiter) of Iona and a good oil with the paint laid on thick and Peploe-esquily.'

Another link between them was the house of Melsetter near Longhope. Stanley had been trained as an architect and worked with Lethaby who had been in charge of restoration and enlargement of Melsetter. Lethaby was a hero of John's and Melsetter was not only of the Betjeman period, late 19th-century, but retained some William Morris-ish features. It is indeed a distinctive house, rather southern in character, built round a courtyard. It might well bear a plaque to the memory of John and Stanley's friendship.

Memoirs (1979)

STANLEY CURSITER – A STROMNESS NEIGHBOUR

HOWIE FIRTH

Even by Orkney standards, where the qualities of neighbourliness in a small community are valued so highly, Stanley Cursiter was one of the best neighbours anyone could wish for. He loved his house by the sea, with its view over the harbour and its regular visitor, the seagull Sigurd, who used to peck the window when it was time for food; but he took a quiet and thoughtful interest in all the activities of the rest of us, and was always ready to help.

When the grass began to grow up between the closely-fitting paving slabs of the pier, Stanley found a kind of hooked implement that was exactly right for scraping it out, and he would be out at work on his own, cleaning up the section of pier of anyone who was away for a while on holiday. He had a supply of grapes from a friend overseas which seemed to arrive just at that time of winter when most of us would go down with a seasonal cold. When my parents were undecided about whether to move to a more convenient house, he suggested how they could expand on the existing site, and went on to make measurements and draw up plans himself, and even produced a plywood model whose exactness of detail made it in after years a much-sought-after doll's house for visiting children.

His concern for others extended naturally to the town of Stromness; he had an architect's eye for detail, and would make suggestions for ways in which the town could best grow, while praising projects of renovation such as the Town Council's work on the houses at the Khyber Pass. He took a great interest in the naming of things, arguing that the simplest name should often be applied, since this would be the name that time would single out – hence Ferry Road.

His comments on the world around were appreciated by the rest of us, on the one hand for his advice and on the other for his observant good humour. When a cautious workman was enlisted to paint the railings at the end of the pier, and began by attaching himself to them with a formidable array of ropes as a safety harness against the sea three feet below, Stanley remarked to us that 'I think we had better have the lifeboat launched – Just In Case.'

Sometimes his conversations would be over a glass of sherry in his living-room, and I remember how fascinated he would be with new ideas, particularly about the natural sciences. On one occasion, he would describe the then newly published book *The Double Helix*, the classic story of the breaking of the genetic code and the discovery of DNA; on another, the concept of a microclimate, and how Orkney's agriculture had been shaped by the combination of sandstone below and the microclimate of land surrounded by ocean.

It was only, however, when I much later listened to the tapes of his radio talks recorded by his friend Ernest Marwick, that I realised that he was just as much of a craftsman with words as in everything else he did. His memories of old Kirkwall, its characters and its cathedral, are classics of their kind, and are one more example of the range of his talent and of his feelings for the islands and people around him. As an artist or an architect, as a writer or a broadcaster, he was indeed a master of all the arts, and my pleasure in these few memories of him is only tempered by the thought that there is so much about the world that I wish I had had the foresight to ask him when I had the chance.

Stanley Cursiter Centenary Exhibition catalogue (1987)

BILLY PEACE THE PROVOST'S DOG

STANLEY CURSITER

I do not have enough science to trace the lineage of Billy. His coat was short, black and shining. He had sharp pointed ears; some distant relative may have been a pug. He was fat, and when I remember him first, his side-whiskers had begun to turn white. He was the Provost's dog, Provost Peace, and as Billy Peace he was known to the whole community. He had survived his master, but something of the dignity and the bearing of the chief magistrate was continued in the dog.

The Provost's house stood at the end of Broad Street, with a small paved courtyard in front. On the line of the street, a high wall closed the courtyard, with an opening in the middle spanned by a light archway. Inside the courtyard, some hint of the 18th century seemed to linger. Billy's favourite corner was at one side of the opening, where he sat leaning against the pillar, his hind legs sticking out a little sideways, as fat dogs' legs do. Before him stretched the Broad Street and the Kirk Green, with the Market Cross in the middle, and at the far end the monument to the Covenanters drowned off the shore of Deerness. Beyond the Kirk Green is the kirkyard and the great mass of the Cathedral, with the ruins of the Bishop's Tower and the palace of the Stewart Earls, and right across from the Cathedral is the Town Hall and the Post Office.

Billy looked out on the visible evidence of centuries of history, and regarded all this as his domain. No dog dared to bark in all this space without the consent of Billy. If a fight started up – even a private fight between two dogs with good reason for difference of opinion – irrespective of the size, shape or colour of the combatants, Billy would leave his corner and charge like a black storm of destruction into the thick of the fray. When he had settled the matter, he returned with dignity to his corner. He was the representative of canine law and order. He perhaps recognised some kinsmanship with the superintendent of police and the two constables. But certain, he never condescended to recognise them as they took their leisured way along the pavement. He was the Provost's dog, and he lived up to the importance of his station.

Billy was no mere blusterer and fighter; he knew the value of strategy. His well-developed figure may have reduced his speed in manoeuvre, but what he lacked in agility, he more than counterbalanced by artfulness. Billy had all a dog's abhorrence of cats; they were a pestilential race, to be chased, harassed, and if possible bitten, on sight. He knew the cat had gifts as a sprinter in the open which gave him little chance, but if Pussy could be chased into a corner of high walls, there were opportunities for a dog to show to advantage. But even there he found that the cat would often jump over him and escape before he had time to change direction. He devised a method of dealing with this trouble. Having chased the cat into a corner, he would reverse and go in backwards, waving his tail at the cat's face. As the cat jumped, Billy jumped, and he usually managed to get in one bite before the cat escaped.

He did not fraternise with the common herd of citizens; he sat leaning against his pillar, his ears cocked, his quick eyes watching the whole street. Most of the townsfolk would say 'Hello, Billy!' as they passed, and they would be favoured with a quick glance. Only for one or two members of the community, there would be a momentary flick of the ears and the tail would give a wag.

But he had one friend, and against all the canons of tradition, it was the postman. John Costie was a fine figure of a man, tall, handsome, with a flowing beard and moustaches, a man who carried his head proudly, and his blue eyes had the flash of his Viking forefathers. When not a postman, he was a shoemaker, and his shop was near the middle of Broad Street. Billy would pay two or three visits to Costie every day, pushing his way in at the door through the shop counter to sit for a minute or two at the feet of his friend, watching him as he strained an upper over a last and drove in the nails to hold it in place; or follow carefully the workings of the double-ended waxed thread as the sole was sewn to the welt. Costie was a fine craftsman with a pride in his work. How often I have seen him, with his head to one side, cast his eye along the lift of an instep or pass his hand caressingly over a toe-cap. A hand-made boot can be nearly as lovely a thing as a boat; and the ship's carpenter and the shoemaker can share the same joy in a well-drawn line.

At that time there were two deliveries of letters in Kirkwall each day. The letters from the South went out late at night or in the early morning, depending on the time of the arrival of the *St Ola* in its crossing of the Pentland Firth. But at four o'clock every afternoon, the local mails were delivered. It was said that Billy sat in the gateway with his eye on the Cathedral clock, and as soon as the hands pointed to four, he made his way to the Upper end of the Post Office Lane. Perhaps it was that he recognised the four strokes on the bell; but every afternoon he was waiting for John Costie when the local mails went out. He would accompany the postman on his round, down the main street past the Big Tree. He would stand at the shop doors with his ears cocked till Costie came out, Minor tours of inspection would be made, for he never neglected his duties as a magistrate. Albert Street, Bridge Street, Shore Street and Catherine Place were all visited; then East Road.

On East Road the space between the houses got wider, and on the East Hill there was open ground. Here for a moment Billy relaxed; he became a dog. Costie would throw stones or sticks, and Billy would run and bark and cast dignity to the winds. But once down the hill and among houses, Billy was again the serious-minded guardian of the town's proprieties.

As Billy got older, he got fatter. The day came when East Road was too steep a hill for the old dog. He would do the half-round and sit at the end of Catherine Place, watching Costie as he went up the road. When the bend at the corner took the postman out of sight, Billy would make his way home. Costie would have to reduce his pace and go slow to let the old dog keep up with him. Then with a pat or two, he would say 'Home, boy,' and the old dog would turn. Billy was always at the end of the lane to meet him at four o'clock, but soon he could only go as far as the Big Tree, and would have to take several rests on the way back.

As Costie would have said, 'That's a while ago noo,' and who knows, in some Dogs' Paradise, Billy may be chasing cats into Elysian corners; and somewhere he may have found another pillar to lean against.

BBC Scotland recording (1965 or 1966)

HINT OF FOREIGN PARTS
IN KIRKWALL

RHODA SPENCE

(Many years after his death, the name of the Scottish writer Lewis Spence is coming back to the fore, through a reviving interest in his work on Celtic mythology and the Atlantis legend. One of his daughters was Claire Kelday, who lived in Orkney for much of her life and contributed greatly to music in the county. Her sister Rhoda followed her father's footsteps in journalism, editing 'Scotland's Magazine' for 23 years and writing many articles, stories and poems for various publications. In her later years, she came to live in Orkney at Eastbank, and she used the time there to good effect, compiling a selection of work into a book, Reading by Lamplight. This is from an early account of a visit to Kirkwall and the impressions it made.)

If anyone mentions Kirkwall to me suddenly, I remember little things like a fuchsia hedge, a milk bottle with a deep head of cream, and a street name plucked from a Viking saga.

Memory, I feel, has not done so badly in hoarding glimpses of homely charm, generosity, and romance from the many aspects of Orkney's county town. Then it really bestirs itself to produce the moment of deepest enchantment. This was when the 'plane first sighted the islands, malachite and amber against the dark sea, and I looked down on the lands which came to Scotland in pledge for a Norwegian princess's dowry.

Comely is the best word to describe Kirkwall's main thoroughfare where I was set down from the airport bus. On the one hand stretches a flagged walk lined by shops and shaded by the famous Big Tree. On the other the road widens to reveal the splendid Cathedral of St Magnus, ember-red in the sunshine. Beyond that it narrows to a diminishing vista of gable ends and crow-steps in pleasantly weathered stone.

There is an intriguing hint of foreign parts, as if some old skipper had come home with tales of Bergen or Danzig, though it is more possibly a folk-memory of the days when Orkney, from being a stepping stone for Viking rule, became a dependency of Norway. Like many people from 'the Sooth' I had not realised till I dipped into Orcadian history that the islands had been under Norway for so long. For centuries Norwegian 'jarls' ruled over a population of mixed Pictish, Norse, and other stock, Norse was spoken, and 'udal' land tenure introduced.

Earl Rognvald was one of those jarls, a brilliant adventurous figure, who took his fleet to the very shores of the Holy Land, yet laid his bones in the great Cathedral of St Magnus which he had founded. He raised the cathedral in memory of his uncle, the good St Magnus, who had been treacherously murdered by his co-ruler Earl Haakon, and showed in his own life that a hero of saga could also be a wise and Christian ruler.

It is one of the most colourful strands in the fringe of British history, and no one who wants to understand Orkney's ghostly ties with Norway should fail to visit the twelfth-century cathedral, where saint and founder are enshrined in massive pillars that once flanked the high altar. At the same time they will see an interior of lofty beauty, matchless between Trondheim and Durham, the older part of which was probably by Durham's architect.

Reading by Lamplight (1991)

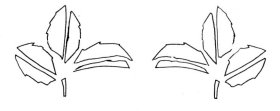

VOICES OF ST MAGNUS CATHEDRAL

ERNEST R. MARWICK

(Ernest Marwick stands out not only for what he achieved in his own right, but for what he did for others — both for individuals and for the community. He systematically gathered a mass of folklore, made many individual tape recordings, published Orkney writers old and new, and worked to preserve the best of the past for a future generation. This is one of the talks he gave on Radio Orkney, a few days before the first St Magnus Festival and a few weeks before his death.)

A number of years ago, when I was visiting in the Norwegian countryside, I found that my host had placed on my bed-table a book called *I Vesterveg*. I skimmed through it and came on a poem entitled *Kirkwall*. I made a copy of the Norwegian and attempted a rough rendering into English. It came back to my mind recently, and I shall read you two of the verses which speak of St Magnus Cathedral:

> *I walk alone in the evening clear*
> *On dear familiar ground,*
> *And voices from the past I hear:*
> *The sound is a living sound...*
> *You men of Agder, from your graves*
> *That Church like a glory springs;*
> *Its tower a sign, above the waves,*
> *To the steadfast heavenly things.*
>
> *The notes die sweetly on the air*
> *Of the bells that mark each hour;*
> *Though dreamy now is the tale they bear,*
> *That Church was an urgent power!*

> *Mighty it was on sea and strand –*
> *Though all forget the past,*
> *It will speak of race and motherland*
> *While its glorious walls shall last.*

The poet, Hans Reynold, did not look on the Cathedral as a mass of stone, but as something magnificently alive.

'There is something in their church,' wrote Storer Clouston as a young man, 'that none of the respectable townsfolk have the slightest suspicion of – something alive that vibrates to the cry of the wind and the breaking of the sea, and the little human events that happen in the crow-stepped houses.'

I feel that, too, every time I go into it … that the Cathedral is filled with a tremendous atmosphere or spirit. In addition, it has, and *has had*, its voices intoning:

> *Ære være Gud i det høieste*
> Glory to God in the highest.

There would have been, too, the sweet boyish voices of the lads in the Sang School, for, as was long since written, the prebend of St Augustine 'wes of auld foundit and provydit for the use and benefite of ane person meit and able to instruct the youth in musick within the burghe of Kirkwall and Cathedral Kirk of Orkney.' Many have thought that the founder and patron of the Cathedral Sang School, whose choristers were trained in it, was none other than St Rognvald himself.

The organ, as a 'voice' of the Cathedral, may seem to us a comparatively new thing, but St Magnus had an organ at least as early as the 1540s. When the noble bishop Robert Reid was Bishop of Orkney he reorganised the constitution of St Magnus Cathedral Chapter. And that Constitution, dated at Kirkwall in 1544, provides that *not only* must the Cathedral have a precentor, but also a 'succentor', 'qualified in both kinds of song, and especially a skilled player on the organ.' He was obliged in the time of the more solemn feasts, as at other services, to play upon the organ the *Te Deum* and the *Benedictus*.

Other 'voices' of the Cathedral have been its bells. What

131

the earliest ones were like we do not know, although one of them may have been the *skellat* bell, now cracked and useless. It was almost certainly cast before the year 1400, and was for generations the town's fire and alarm bell. Its shrill voice was suitable for that, and also for calling out schoolboys and apprentices in the early morning. How they must have hated its clatter!

The three bells we still use were made in 1528 for Bishop Maxwell, whose close friend King James Fifth instructed the cannon-maker Robert Borthwick to cast the bells in the cannon foundry of Edinburgh Castle. The greatest of them weighs over fourteen hundredweights, and all three – tenor, bourdon and treble – are rung by one person, pulling the ropes with both hands and a foot.

For a while in the 1960s and early 1970s the bells were mute on Sundays, for we had no bell-ringer, so a tape-recording was used instead. Now, glory be, we have a guild of bell-ringers, and thanks to them the fine old bells are ringing again.

The curfew bell, perhaps the most characteristic 'voice' of the Cathedral, as heard from outside, rings for five minutes each evening, beginning one minute after the clock has struck eight o'clock.

Since 1925, the Cathedral has had a magnificent 'voice' in the rich-sounding and versatile Willis organ, with over 2,000 pipes; and it has been excellently served by its organists, and by a choir which is rapidly becoming famous. But one of the things that keeps it alive and vibrant, and that would have delighted Earl Rognvald, its founder, who invited poets and musicians to his Court in Kirkwall, is that in our own day new modes of expression have been welcomed in the Cathedral – singers, orchestras, drama. Now, fresh voices are to celebrate, in the very newest music, the man and the event out of which the Cathedral took its being.

And surely this continuing celebration of Magnus – from the medieval hymns to the modern music of Peter Maxwell Davies – is a wonderful thing!

BBC Radio Orkney (June 1977)

THE BLACKSMITH'S SHOP

FREDDIE GIBSON

(If you have a rusted mass of metal and wonder about the engine that it once was, contact Orkney Vintage Club. Their pool of skills, energy and enthusiasm encapsulates all that is best in the great Orcadian fascination with machinery. Presiding over a vast juggernaut of an engine you will find Freddie, one of the Club's most active members, with a fund of stories for all occasions, as here in his account of tales from the blacksmith's shop of his apprentice days.)

The ringing anvil, the fire and the ever-open door must have been like a magnet to everybody going past the blacksmith's shop because we had a constant stream of visitors. We did not stop work just because someone came in to pass the time of day and, after they had warmed their hands, they would drift out to be replaced by somebody else. Just before teatime and on Wednesday afternoons, when the shops had a half-day, we always seemed to have a few more visitors. I once read somewhere that nothing said in a blacksmith shop was admissible as evidence in a court of law.

I had been at the shop a few weeks when the boss said he was going out and left me with some work to do at the bench. He had been gone about five minutes when a chap called Willie came into the ship with about six feet of light chain over his shoulder. He said he wanted it annealed but that he could do himself. I put the stroup back into the tuyere, blew up the fire and left him to it. He raked out the centre of the fire, made a ball out of the chain and laid it in the middle, then raked all the coal back on top and started pumping the bellows. I thought that that was a funny way to do it but he seemed very self-assured so I left him to it and went back to the bench. A bit later, when I looked round, the fire was just like a big sparkler and I knew that there was something wrong. I was halfway across the floor when John, a retired engineer from up the road, came in.

'A new blacksmith?' he said, 'and I'll tell you something. You'll need to get whatever you have in the fire out quick.'

I think that this time Willie was beginning to think there was something wrong. He stopped blowing, shoved the poker in the fire and lifted out a sparkling white lump that had once been a length of chain but was now only recognisable by a few unburnt links around the outside.

'You have made a right mess of that,' said John, 'but it serves you right. I always said that you would never come to any good, especially after you rescued the mummy's foot.' And with that John went out leaving Willie and me looking at the rapidly cooling lump of metal. The colder it got, the worse it looked, and to cheer him up I said that we could find another bit of chain.

Just with that the boss came in and Willie told him the story. We found a bit of chain, annealed it for him and, when the boss asked him why he wanted it annealed, he said there was no special reason, it just looked good on the bill.

Willie was a self-employed carpenter who did a lot of work for the Harbour Commissioners, the shipping companies and the local boats. His workshop and yard stood exactly where Croy's petrol pumps stand today. In his younger days he had gone to sea as a ship's carpenter and was always good for a story. After he went away, I was telling the boss what happened and I asked what the significance was regarding John's remarks about the mummy's foot.

At one time there was a druggist's shop in Bridge Street (a druggist's shop sold patent medicine and was not allowed to make up prescriptions), and the proprietor had a mummified foot in a glass case above his desk which stood in a corner of the shop. John was very friendly with with the druggist but every time he went into the shop he got on about the foot, telling him it was a disgusting thing to have on show and he should keep it out of sight. John got so worked up about it that he offered to buy it and eventually made the druggist an offer he could not refuse. After leaving the shop with his purchase, he tied it up in a brown paper parcel, then made his way down to Ritchie's Slip. Here, he selected a flat stone, parcelled the lot together and proceeded to the point of the pier where one of the local smacks was getting ready to sail for Leith. John gave the mate a shout, slipped him half-a-crown and instructed him to drop the parcel over the side when they got to the Pentland Skerries. As soon as John's back was turned, the mate dropped the parcel over the side, as he would have other things to think about by the time he reached the Pentland Skerries.

Before the war, there were still a few rich people in Orkney who could afford yachts and, in the winter, they were drawn up in a noust out along the Grain Shore. Willie had been instructed to go out and do some repairs on one of them and, after he crossed the eye, he cut down to the grassy bank at the top of the beach. He had not gone very far when he thought he saw something lying in the ebb. He left his tool-bass on the bank and walked out to investigate. The brown paper had not lasted long and the stone had not been very securely tied, but the foot had survived its dip. Willie had heard the story and recognised the foot, but John was not very pleased when he next visited Willie's workshop and saw the foot had pride of place on the wall above the fire. No amount of pleading, threatening or swearing was going to make Willie give up his prize. He told John that he could not remember whether it was flotsam or jetsam but he had taken the best legal advice available in Kirkwall and he had been assured that it was his to do with whatever he wanted.

Many years later, I was in Orkney for a holiday when I met Willie outside the Shore Dues Office. He greeted me and asked how I was getting on, what I was doing and where I was working. When I told him I was working in Leith, he asked about his old haunts around the Docks – The Sailor's Home, Ross's Bar, The Corn Exchange, The Steam Boat, The Bay Horse, The Carrier's Quarters, Mother Aitken's and The King's Wark (better known as The Jungle). I was all ears when

Willie said. 'I'll tell you a story about Leith.'

I came home from deep-sea and was standing right here when cousin John came along and asked if I would come down to Leith with him as he was a man short and was sailing next morning. He was skipper of a smack and was a very good man who never did anything stupid so I said I would go. The first night ashore in Leith I met a very nice girl and ended up spending a few days ashore. I had an uneventful trip back to Kirkwall, spend a day so at home, and went back deep-sea.

I was not back in Orkney for ten years, but it was a repeat of the previous time. I was standing here again when cousin John came up to me, a man short and sailing next morning and would I go with him? This was winter time but the weather was settled so I said that I would go. There was a lot of snow on the ground as we tied up at the Shore in Leith and, all of a sudden, I got a big wet snowball right on the back of my neck.

I looked around and saw three little boys on the quay. I jumped ashore and caught the smallest one.

'What's your name?'

'*I'm no' telling you.*'

'Where do you live?'

'*I'm no' telling you.*'

'What's your fathers name?'

'*Willie ——, Ship's Carpenter, Kirkwall.*'

I let him go, jumped back on board and never went ashore again all the time we were in Leith and I've never been back since.

A good story which was well worth the pint and the four fingers of the Owld Kirk that I set up when the Queen's Hotel opened.

'Oxy, Cocoa, RO and a Few Others', *Orkney Vintage Club Newsletter No.* 7 (1990)

THE SHOEMAKER IN KIRKWALL

JIMMY HARRISON

(Jimmy Harrison had his own shoemaking business in the Strynd for many years. His early apprenticeship had been with the firm Dundee Equitable Depot in Albert Street (the modern D&E Shoe Shop). His description of those days was amongst the accounts gathered together by Sheila Spence in 1988 in the book Old Orkney Trades._)_

The shoemaker stood at the bench for hammering and cutting work, but sat for sewing. Each man had his own wooden stool – often made by himself. It had no back, and the wooden seat was slightly bevelled to give more comfort. Two drawers were down one side of it and were used for storing hemp etc. On the other side was a kind of extended arm, consisting of a tray on which lay awls and rosit. Also on this arm was fixed a stout piece of leather with a slit in it. Into this slit would be pushed the candle used to warm the heel-iron, which would be placed on a block of any suitable size and height, so that it was over the top of the candle flame. The space under the stool was used for storing personal effects, such as the hand leather worn when stitching. The first stool which I had was inherited from a previous owner – probably several previous owners as the seat had worn through into a hole which was filled with a cushion.

The shoemaker's shop was very much a social centre – especially my own shop in the Strynd. Frequently children, on their way to and from school, would come in to watch for a while. Adults came in during the day and in the evening, when I would often be working until nine or ten o'clock at night. Some came in with work, others to exchange the latest news, and many said that they liked the smell of leather about the place. Towards the end of my working life I served on Kirkwall Town Council, and from the large cross-section of the public who visited my premises I felt that I was in a very good position to assess public opinion on local matters which arose during Council meetings.

As well as shoemaking I did a small amount of saddlery – mostly the making of bridles. For several years I made the ba' used in the Christmas and New Year Ba' Games in Kirkwall. The ba's were usually made either by the saddlers or shoemakers of Kirkwall. The main difference between the hand stitching done by saddlers and that done by shoemakers is that the saddler uses a needle for sewing and a straight awl for making the holes, whereas the shoemaker uses the flexible biss and the bent awl. It can be seen then that the curved shape and awkward angles of the ba' could be done more easily by the tools of the shoemaker. It also meant that the packing-hole made by the shoemaker could be finished off with concealed stitching, whereas that made by the saddler had to be covered over with a leather plate and external stitching.

Some of the earlier ba' makers took home ready-made leather football cases and adapted them, but the style of ba' which I made was a spherical ba' made up of seven hand-sewn panels. It could be machine-stitched, but hand sewing was considered stronger in view of the tuction that it would have to withstand during the course of the game. Good-quality box-calf leather was the choice material, as it was strong yet stretchy. It had to be carefully selected so that one panel of the ba' did not stretch more than another when being packed. All the seams of the panels, with piping between each, were hand-stitched together using 5-ply hemp coated with rosit, leaving a small opening at the top between two panels. Through this hole the packing would be put in.

The packing was cork dust obtained from local fruiterers and greengrocers, who took home barrels of grapes packed in this material. The ba' was packed very firmly and tightly, the cork dust being packed in with the aid of a pointed stick, which had been carefully smoothed and rounded to prevent damage to the leather. Working was made easier if the leather was kept damp during the making, and particularly during the packing. The dampness made the leather more stretchy, and when it did dry out the ba' was then even more firm and hard. Between two and three buckets of cork dust went into one ba'. All the stitching was on the inside and, to finish, the filling hole was closed with two or three stitches inside the fold of the piping, and the panel seam and the seam pressed down to conceal the stitches.

The ba' was now a perfectly even seven-panelled sphere, with no external seams or projections which might catch or tear or be used as a grip during the game. It was finished by dyeing each alternate panel black, leaving the other panels a natural brown, and finally giving the whole ba' a fine polished finish. When ready for play the men's ba' was about 28 inches in circumference and weighed about 3lb. The boys' ba' was slightly smaller in circumference and weighed about 2lb.

Old Orkney Trades (1988)

STORIES BEHIND THE BA'

GORDON LINKLATER

(A native of Kirkwall, Gordon Linklater served in the Royal Navy in wartime, and subsequently the Customs service in Orkney and London. He divides his retirement between gardening, golf, and providing a fund of stories of Orkney life to the local media.)

Every year, early in December, the citizens of the ancient City and Burgh of Kirkwall notice, in certain windows of business establishments along the main streets, ba's that will be played for on the forthcoming Christmas and New Year's Days. Many give little thought to where they have come from and who has done all the necessary organisation. They all appear as by magic but the truth is that there isn't any magic involved.

The Ba' is unique for two reasons. Firstly it must be the only event now in Orkney where the organisers haven't gone cap in hand to the Council asking for handouts of some kind. People in Kirkwall have always put their hands in their pockets and subscribed, some a little and some a lot. The making of the ba's is costing more each year and the Ba' committee welcomes any donation, large or small. Secondly, it must also be the only event anywhere in the county that starts on the stroke of the hour stated.

The Ba' in Kirkwall hasn't always found favour with certain circles and there have been various moves to have the event banned. Permission for the Ba' to take place has only been granted by a small majority of the Council on occasion. The most excellent books *Uppies and Doonies* and *The Ba' 1945-59* are a mine of information on the subject and are compulsory reading for all enthusiasts.

Before the last war James Nicholson, known as 'Nicky,'

undertook the collection of the money necessary to pay for the ba's. He was most successful in approaching local business men such as P. C. Flett, John Sclater the draper and others who donated freely. He once decided that he would spread his net a little further and accompanied by his schoolgirl daughter, Jenny, now Mrs G. Johnson, he tried to collect door to door. The police suddenly appeared and took both of them down to the Police Station on the Back Road. They warned the now tearful Jenny and her father that proceedings would be taken against them if they persisted in door to door collections. Perhaps this episode spoiled his enthusiasm for organising the Ba' as, after the war, he contented himself by obtaining previously won ba's to continue the game, and then quietly stepping aside. The collection of old trophies had become necessary anyway, because leather was hard to get and was expensive. The old ones served the purpose, and rejuvenated and polished up by Jim Harrison they served admirably.

In the early 1950's there were complaints that certain women were interfering in the Boys' Ba'. This was something that had always occurred but was never really troublesome. It was understandable that mothers, aunts and sisters always wanted to see fair play and also to protect their little 'darlings.' The Ba' committee decided, however, that the next Ba' should be monitored by at least two members. Jim Harrison and I, being then founder members, were delighted to attend and deal with the problem. It must be remembered, and obvious, that a lady of thirteen or fourteen stone is more than a match for a lad of fourteen. Jim and I duly attended at the appointed time and realized that, far from the ladies interfering, the police were the worst offenders. They were deciding the direction in which the Ba' would go, no sticking in certain doorways or down certain lanes. Tradition had always been that the police stood well back and would only 'pick up the pieces,' as it were. Shortly before the war, however, the police force in Orkney had been reorganised and had come under the control of Scottish police regulations. A Chief Constable was appointed and many of the new type policemen were not locals.

We asked the police to step back and let things take their course but they were reluctant to relinquish their authority. Jim Harrison, well known for his reticence and demure demeanor, suddenly let go a string of oaths, letting the police know in no uncertain terms what their conduct should be. The result of this was that Jim and I were ushered up to the corner of Spence's shop, to be confronted by the Chief Constable who told us if we didn't behave and allow the police to keep order, he would forbid the Ba' to be played in future.

At that threat Jim lost control and, with a volley, vilified the police and everybody in authority. The Chief Constable then gave Jim a verbal warning that if he didn't behave he would be charged with a breach of the peace. Whereupon Jim let forth another volley.

'Don't be so-and-so daft, the Toon Council gives permission for the Ba', no you, and the whole thing's a breach of the peace. I'm a Toon Coonciller,' he yelled, 'I'll end up in the Burgh Coort next week fining me'sel ten bob.'

The Chief Constable saw the funny side of it and cleared us off, but the police stayed well back after that.

The Ba' players, both Uppies and Doonies, were never bitter enemies. Maybe harsh words were spoken in the heat of the moment but after all we worked, lived and socialised together, so no hard feelings were carried over. It is said there aren't any rules, but there are – the normal courtesy shown to opponents in any game and the avoidance of physical damage to anyone.

Once at the Ba', not long after it was thrown up, someone grabbed my trouser pocket and nearly ripped the right leg right off. It required two hands to keep me covered and avoid arrest for indecent exposure. I would have to go home and change, wasting valuable playing time. Tom Sclater, an avid Uppie and opponent, say my predicament and asked his wife to go upstairs to their home in the Town Hall and find a pair of trousers that I could wear. Mrs Sclater went willingly. I believe she is a closet Doonie, originating from the North Isles. She came back with a pair so that I could continue playing.

There was a mention a short time ago that women had little to do with the Ba' except to throw up the Boys' ba'. Older readers will remember the Women's Ba' just after the last war, a disaster that will never be repeated. The ladies went berserk, punching and hairpulling and other unladylike behaviour. One reason women aren't usually asked to throw up the Men's ba' is that the ba' is a lot larger and heavier than the boys'. Throwing from the Mercat Cross onto the street is a considerable distance and the ba' striking the forecourt or dyke, bouncing up and down, would cause an advantage to one side or the other. Of course, there isn't anything to prevent someone throwing up the ba' coming closer to the street in line with the Cross, there aren't supposed to be any rules! On occasion some men haven't had the strength to clear the dyke, resulting in a dangerous scramble as players and spectators become embroiled, some to grab the ba' and some to get out of the way.

Sadly, when Sydney Garrioch, the saddler who made ba's along with his father, died, it caused a dilemma as to who should make ba's. Fortunately, committee member Jim Harrison was a shoemaker and volunteered to have a go, providing we all helped in the packing. Packing was extremely important as ba's had to be iron hard to stand up to the 'tuction' of the actual game. It was a hard, slow process, requiring strength and stamina and was painful on the hands and arm muscles. Mrs Garrioch approached us with the information that her husband had partially completed two ba's before he died, and would they be acceptable if she completed them. They were completed but the committee rejected them because they considered they weren't hard enough. Mrs Garrioch was compensated for her work, and that solves the mystery why six ba's were made in one year. Perhaps now, with modern machinery, some female will be able to sew and pack ba's to the standard required, and allow further contribution from the distaff side.

On one occasion a lady was considered to throw up the Men's ba' and it fell to me to make the arrangements. Meeting this lady's husband on the street, I thought it would be a good idea to sound out if she would be willing to do the honour. On putting the question, I was met with a torrent of abuse. His wife wasn't going to be associated with such a rabble and in no circumstances would he allow such a thing. Never again in my time on the committee was a woman, married or single, ever considered for such an honour.

One thing a member of the committee must see to is picking up the ba' from the place of display and giving it to the person who is going to throw it up. On one occasion it was my turn. The ba' was the Boys' New Year one and Dougie Shearer was to throw it up. Dougie asked if I would deliver the ba' to him in plenty of time, as he thought he might sleep in. I readily agreed because I had learned my lesson before this time and didn't partake too much on the Hogmanay so as to be fit for the Men's Ba'. Next morning I awoke with a start and, looking at the clock, thought I'd slept in. 'It's already ten o'clock,' I gasped, threw on some clothes, and, grabbing the ba', rushed out. At that time I lived in Laing Street on the balcony at the back, and in my hurry I went headlong down the steps, got up and on to the street, and fell again. The ba' shot from my grasp down Laing Street and right down Pork Horne's lane.

By this time, between pain and anxiety, tears started to form and, grabbing the ba' once more, I rushed up the street. Reaching Leith the butchers, I saw that there was no-one in Broad Street. Thinking, 'Good God, everyone has got fed up waiting and gone home,' thoughts then went through my mind of catching the *St Ola* the next day or even suicide. I walked up Broad Street and looking up at the Kirk clock saw that it was only eight o'clock! Getting back home I found my wife had been alarmed by the speed and commotion I had caused getting dressed and racing out. On hearing my story she thought it was hilarious and the laugh of the year.

The Orkney View (December 1994/January 1995)

UPPIES AND DOONIES

JOHN D. M. ROBERTSON

(John Robertson has two highly successful careers, which have made him well-known outside Orkney. As a businessman, he has developed the family company of S. & J. D. Robertson into a major Scottish oil distributor which supplies not only most of the Highlands and Islands but also the Falkland Islands. In public life, he has been in demand for many years to serve on government bodies at a local and national level. These major demands on his time have limited his opportunities to pursue his third field of interest, the writing of local history, but he has still been able over the years to produce some fine work, in particular in the book Uppies and Doonies. His eye for detail and gift for narrative are demonstrated in these extracts.)

The Ba' is played irrespective of weather conditions, and New Year's Day 1967 was bitterly cold, with the additional discomfort of a strong North-West gale. After a protracted contest in which play surged as far up as Gunn's Close, the scrum was eventually forced down Great Western Road and Burnmouth Road, and shortly before six o' clock the interlocked mass of men spilled over the sea wall and on to the open shore in front of the Ayre Houses. The scene was memorable, with a knot of claimants and their attendant supporters grappling in the wintry sea, while the gale drove blinding flurries of snow and hail straight in off the bay. In these Arctic conditions dozens of hardy players struggled, sometimes waist deep in the breakers, at other times ploughing through banks of rotting seaweed, and it took twenty minutes of animated argument on the wild darkened shore before the winner was chosen. Only then did soaked, battered players and frozen spectators take refuge from the storm.

A century before, on New Year's Day 1866, the game took place in a snowstorm in the presence of a good number of spectators who could see nothing 'on account of the blinding snowdrift. A dense cloud surcharged with whirling blasts of snow and hail, overspread the town about the time appointed for the commencement of the game.' The contest was a short one, but was played throughout under these severe conditions.

Whether one is an Uppie or a Doonie is determined by place of birth and indeed some families have mixed loyalties. An amusing story is told of a diehard Uppie father-to-be who, when the termination of his wife's pregnancy approached, would on no account allow her to stray below the Mercat Cross! One day to his consternation he came upon her in Albert Street, and shepherding her well above the Cross, he chided: 'Noo, noo, lass, we kinno tak the risk o' hivan a blinkan Doonie in wir hoose.'

A Doctor Russell had a practice in Kirkwall for some years, and he was an enthusiastic player, winning a ba' around 1895. Apparently one Christmas Day, Mrs Russell, who certainly was not a devotee of the game, thought that the time had come to put an end to her husband's annual foolishness, and marched him off to the Episcopal Church. This in no way damped the good doctor's zest for the contest, and after the service he went straight to the game. There, handing his tile hat and gold-topped malacca cane to a spectator, and still clad in frock coat, he plunged into the fray. In the course of play one of the contestants broke a leg, and was removed to the side while help was summoned. A perspiring and dishevelled Doctor Russell emerged from the scrum, set the man's leg on the barrow where he was lying and, duty done, rejoined the struggle.

This story was related to me by Mr Stanley Cursiter who is the proud possessor of a miniature ba' – perfectly made and given to him seventy-five years earlier by the late John Costie, Shoemaker, Main Street, Kirkwall. Mr Cursiter told me that in 1895 Mr Costie was paid about 30s. for making a ba'. This was quite a sum of money then, and gives a good idea of the amount of work required for each Costie ba'.

Sometimes the game debouches into lanes and back gardens, the precise location of the ba' is unknown, and complete confusion reigns. Players and spectators run helter-skelter in the general mix up, and this can lead to amusing incidents and an unusual game. An example of this occurred on Christmas Day 1934, when at Gunn's Close the ba' was thrown into a garden and the players spilled in after it. Swarming through into an adjoining vegetable bed the scrum created havoc before it was finally broken up, and the ba' brought out and thrown up again on the main road. Meanwhile more than half the players and at least a hundred spectators rushed up to Victoria Street where an alarming rumour met them that the ba' had been smuggled, and was well on its way to the Harbour. The crowd streamed down to Broad Street where the grave news was that the smuggler had been given a lift by a motor cyclist and was heading out the Ayre Road. The pack set out in pursuit, and an innocent incoming motorist was stopped and ordered to surrender the ba'! Then 'for some minutes the crowd patrolled the Ayre Road and Harbour Street, and was coming to the conclusion that all was over when a courier came hastening down Junction Road to impart the startling news that the game was still going strong in the neighbourhood of the Crafty. The hoaxed crowd, with renewed enthusiasm, proceeded to the scene of combat, where a sadly depleted gallery was watching two even more sadly depleted teams fighting for supremacy at the Saverock Creamery. There were less than thirty players, about fourteen aside, taking part in the game.'

A clever and unusual tactic occurred in the New Year's Day game 1901. Play had reached the doorway of what was then known as Charlie MacGregor's shop – the last building at the top of Broad Street. An Uppie called Bob Nicolson pretended to be injured, and as he stood in the doorway clutching himself the scrum ground past. Play continued some yards away, and unnoticed, Nicolson, another stalwart named Billy Wick, and the ba' went their unmolested way to the Uppie goal. Incidentally when these two players were proceeding up Victoria Street a lady came out of her house and casually asked how the game was going. Nicolson nonchalantly lifted his jersey, showed the trophy and said, 'The ba's right here.' In a deserted street with the clamour of the game a hundred yards back, the scene must have been memorable, even slightly unreal.

After the game was over came a most unkind cut, when the players discovered they could neither celebrate their victory nor drown their disappointment. The publicans had decided to have a half-holiday but had given no intimation to the public!

There is a curious story told about a game played in the dim past in which the ba' was never taken to either of the goals, and the tale revolves round the friendship of two men – an Uppie and a Doonie. Apparently during the course of the game the Doonie slipped away unnoticed with the ba', and his Uppie friend who was late, chanced to meet him in Mill Street. Neither man would betray his Ba' loyalty but neither wanted to endanger the life-long friendship, so they agreed to hide the ba' and lose it forever. This they did, and the game was never finished. The story is given a tinge of authenticity by the fact that many years ago a very old four-panelled ba', partly decomposed, was found hidden away in the rafters of a stable in Kirkwall.

Uppies and Doonies (1967)

TWENTY DOONIES IN THE BASIN

DAVID HORNE

(The ba', with its lack of formal rules, is about as unlike the game of cricket as you can get, but the reports of the ba' have inspired writing that can stand comparison with the truly great cricket writers. Maybe the pauses, while the mass of bodies push and heave and the ba' stays put for a while, provide the opportunity for the kind of reflective thought that provides such pleasure to cricket commentators. Whatever the reason, the ba' reports in The Orkney Herald of David Horne of Kirkwall, who wrote under the pen-name 'Cubbie Roo,' read like pure poetry. There are the thumb-nail sketches of the personalities, and roll-calls of names that should be read out like the text of 'Under Milk Wood.' The play ebbs and flows like the stanzas in a ballad, and particular themes recur in a regular refrain. It's not surprising that David Horne was also a musician. We join the 1948 Christmas Day ba' just by the Big Tree, at 1.30 pm, in brilliant december sunshine, with the Doonies beginning to feel, in the words of the reporter, that 'today the ba' has the smell of salt water.')

Uppie 'Titto' Linklater, coalman, strives to stem the tide. More faces – Andrew Thomson, 'Tiny' Leonard, plumber; Ian Smith, coalman; young 'Banffie' George Ritchie; Alan Wylie; Dougie Campbell.

She's at MacDonald's the butchers, and is getting 'coorser.' Many more doonies who had not intended to take part, here lend their weight.

Five minutes more and she's at Morgan's the jeweller's and then bounds across to Boots, the chemists' (Wright's). A B.E.A. 'plane flies low overhead to get a good view. Several players fall, but are quickly pulled to their feet by willing hands.

There is no 'smuggling' – no lightning 'break-aways.'

She reaches the Atholl Cafe railings and we notice with forebodings that Davie does not have his windows very strongly barricaded.

Sutherland Taylor's son Sid is there; Bobbo Sinclair from the Cheese Factory; Peter Johnstone; young Arnold Russell from Cannigall who was in the boys' ba'; big Hercus, the Edayman off the 'Sigurd'; old ba' player Peter Hercus, wistfully looking on; Jeemie Maxwell, who spent some years 'down-under.'

She stops with a bump at the Albert Kinema. I run upstairs to lean out of Dougie Shearer's window for a bird's eye view.

Old doonie stalwart Bill Lennie is a keen onlooker. Dennis Linklater of Bill Reid's is in the thick of her; big 'Danno' Johnstone fain would have a go; Russell Croy, of the Rovers, sticks in with the best of them; Jim 'Pluto' Shearer; 'Pym' Sinclair; George Robinson from Aim's Buildings.

A rumour goes round that she's been pushed through one of the Albert Kinema's windows – but it's only a ruse.

Jacky Crisp, docker, is playing today, and Davie Wylie; Billy Peace of Picky; young Pat Baikie and Alan Rosie the linesman.

Two o'clock. Back to the Atholl Cafe. There is little pressure in the middle, however, for all her size. Down to the Dundee Equitable.

Then Jimmy Monkman breaks clear and runs off with her down-street – doubling on his tracks, but he's caught and she's back at the Dundee.

Sammy Bews, policeman, off-duty, is pushing down. Up she goes a bit again.

Our forecast is correct. A window of the Atholl Cafe goes in with a tinkle of falling glass and a player hands out a plate of fancies to the crowd. Soon home-bakes are being handed out indiscriminately, a wag remarking, 'Shae disna waant tae go bye the Atholl. Davie's fancies are too good.'

Over to the Picture House again. Here footballer John Donaldson gets her away but the street is too packed to go far.

More kent faces are seen. David Bews, apprentice joiner; Gordon Muir of the Auction Mart; Alex Wilson of the Power Station; Bob Gunn, docker, and John Sinclair, joiner.

Steam rises. Back to the Atholl. Over to J. & J. Smith's – oldest draper shop in Kirkwall.

Jim Miller of the Post Office helps at the edges. 'Blurt' Rosie is there and young 'Juker' Bews; 'Bobbo' Thomson and young Bob Gunn.

Policeman Sammy Bews lifts out splinters of glass from the broken window. The cold wind makes the spectators shiver.

More tinkling of glass. Another Cafe window is broken. The time is 2.20 pm. Up she goes again to Wright's. Jocky Sinclair gets the soles and heels torn right off his shoes. The shrill cries of the bairns, 'Come on the uppies' and 'Doon wi' her, doonies' never let up.

Jim Bews, the Shapinsay footballer, pushes doon; Bob Muir is there and Dougie Leslie; Fred Johnstone; Gordon Cooper, the milkman, still wearing his cap; Ian Fraser, redoubtable young uppie; George Louttit, docker, trombone player and lover of 'swing'; 'Tullie' Tullock, Ford's Orkney agent; schoolboy David Tinch; Bill Rorie.

She's back at J. & J. Smith's.

Here Alan Rosie is lifted bodily over the heads of the uppies.

Up to the Cafe again; across to Wright's. Up to Morgan's in short, quick rushes.

More players are discerned. Arthur Borwick of Tafts; Tom Foubister of Croy's Garage; Billy Barnett; Ian Swanney.

A man from Banffshire, who has been playing up valiantly, thinks the game terrific but that the folk south should be told more about it. 'Rugby is nothing to this,' he says.

It is a quarter to three.

Three Hatston soldiers in their best rig enter the game and play down. Over to the Kinema and 'Pingo' senior nearly works the oracle. Up the close between the cafe and Groundwater's shop. Someone loses an iron heel. Listen again to the 'song of the ba'.'

Further up Groundwater's close for a rest. 'Ginger' Wylie from Burgher's Bay – still with only half-a-shirt – does his stuff; an Edinburgh girl student excitedly cries, 'Up wi' her, uppies.' Another uppie girl supporter remarks, 'My I wid love to gae a push.' And in she goes and puts her wish into action.

Big Bob Craigie the policeman is caught in a doonie rush and momentarily loses his hat – but enjoys the fun.

She's down at Leith's the butchers. Enters the opening between Davie Nicolson's and Flett's Home Bakery. A welcome rest for a breather and smoke.

Johnny Walls, his throat parched, says to Davie Nicolson (through the window), 'Gae's a drink o' watter min.' Which was the best joke of the day.

Out with a rush to Hourston's the jeweller's; across to the bakery; down the 'Orkney Herald' Lane a bit; along to Drever & Heddle's. Time 3.10 pm. Over to Turfus's; back to Drever & Heddle's; some bairns are on the wall there and are hanging on to the railings.

A high-pitched wail and they disappear as part of the railings fall into the courtyard, but nobody is hurt. More for the Council to put right.

Moving down, she turns into 'Porky Horne's Lane' and sticks for a minute. As she passes the bacon-curer's, Sgt. Vickers (Hatston) – who had been all dolled up in his kilt but who wanted to 'have a go' and borrowed a pair o' breeks – shouts, 'A pound of ham.'

Past the Albert Hotel, through the narrow lane at the back. She stops – and the third window-pane goes. A yell, 'She's in the hotel.'

The game breaks up. Folk run here, there and everywhere. Nobody knows where the ba' is. Too bad for the doonies if she should go up after all.

Gerald Eccles runs up the Back Road, shouting 'She's awey upstreet. Doodles Crisp has her.' But the doonies are not to be deceived. I enter the hotel to find out where she is. 'She wis here but she's no' here noo.' A couple of doonies also enter but can't find her. We come out. The ba' is raging as fiercely as ever at 'Long' John Miller's show-room window.

'Doodles' – I find out later – went in through the broken window shoulder first, after having thrown in the ba' first. Jocky Sinclair caught hold of his feet as he lay over the sill. Then he let go and the last he saw was 'Doodles' wrestling with Tom Brough on a bed for possession of the ba'.

Edwin Work, the ironmonger, is in her; and Jim Kelday, former butcher, now G.P.O. linesman; Jim Duncan, postman; young Billy Grant from the Ayre Mills; Dod Donaldson, the butcher, and eldest son George, the swimmer; John Flett of P. C. Flett & Co.; Billy Cooper, the baker; Billy Wilson; Leslie Leonard; and many, many more, the names of whom have slipped my memory.

Time 3.40 pm. It is getting dark but still the uppies will not give in. But the writing is on the wall and the ba' will soon be in the water. And not a single uppie will grudge the doonies their win.

Long John Miller is caught here but likes it and decides to stay where he is. She makes for the Basin. A rush round the Kiln Corner at breakneck speed – towards the iron railings at the harbour. I jump aboard a fishing boat tied up at the West Pier. The tide – fortunately – is out and there is only a few feet of water.

Down the small slipway from the head of the West Pier she goes with a rumble of tired feet. The players can't stop in time. They waver on the edge of the slipway and there is a hush as first one, and then another, tumbles or is pushed into the sea until, with a mighty splashing of water and spumes of spray, there are close on twenty bobbing up and down in the icy-cold Basin, the ba' somewhere in their midst.

Tom Brough has her but Danno Grieve wants 'Tucker' Miller to get her. There is some squabbling. She is thrown up the slipway to be caught and handed to the happy 'Tucker,' who is at once shouldered high up the slip to the Harbour Front. The score or so droukled players squelsh and chirp their way home, leaving a trail of salt-water behind them, and the rest of the players and spectators go home, too, to waiting dinners – the lucky few to hot baths.

And none of the men who took a dip will even get a cold, far less catch pneumonia. They're tough, mighty tough in Orkney.

The time is ten minutes to four o'clock. The 1948 Christmas Day Men's Ba' is over.

The Orkney Herald (December 1948)

FEAST DAYS

JOHN FIRTH

(John Firth was born at Estaben in Redland, in the parish of Firth, in 1838. He served his time as a journeyman and set up his own business in Finstown as a joiner, later developing the making of handmills. In 1920, when he was 82 and still working, his book, Reminiscences of an Orkney Parish, was published, putting on record a complete picture of the way of life of his native parish.)

Though the time was changed in the year 1752, Orcadians held to the old style, which was twelve days later. Even within forty years back, one old resident in Finstown stuck tenaciously to old Yule Day and old New Year's Day.

Preparations for these feast days were made by baking scones, brewing ale, and by taking in an extra quantity of peats on Yule Even, the peaty neuk being filled up to the rafters with a supply sufficient to last over New Year's Day. On Yule Day no work was done, the day being spent in visiting and treating. If open weather, one or two of the old men made a pilgrimage in the early morning to the top of the hill, to see if any trace of frost could be found, for a green Yule augured ill for the health of the community. A dance for the young people was held in the evening, all returning to their homes for supper, for that was the event of the day. The other meals of the day consisted of the usual cheese and bread accompanied with ale, but there was always 'flesh' for supper.

The advent of New Year's Day was heralded by the young people going from house to house singing the New Year's Song, and this was kept up until a late date. First-footing, still in fashion, was accompanied with nettle-burning. The meaning or origin of the latter custom the writer never heard, but it was very common practice. Young folk were on the outlook for some time previous, and great secrecy was kept regarding the whereabouts of a good fresh bunch of nettles. Of course he was the victor who could strike the foremost blow, but it was not allowable to touch the face, only the hands and feet. Some wily ones, rising early on New Year's morning, secreted the nettles underneath the blankets, whereupon the sleeper, on giving a morning stretch, received a severe burn on his feet coming in contact with the noxious weed. Otherwise the day was passed in much the same style as Christmas Day, only with the addition of ba'-playing for the men and boys, and for others the tamer amusement of weighing, all and sundry repairing to the barn of the licensed maltster or the miller, to learn how many pounds avoirdupois they had gained or lost since last New Year's Day.

Other feasts and holidays held by the people in old times have now passed into oblivion. Aphelly Day came in the end of January, and was observed, like New Year's Day, by feasting and ba'-playing.

The quarter days were Candlemas, Beltane, Lammas and Hallowmas. The airt of the wind on the quarter days betokened the direction of the prevailing winds during that quarter. The weather of Candlemas and Beltane days received particular attention, and even yet one hears it referred to in a jocular manner:

> *'If the lavroo' sings afore Candlemas Day,*
> *Sheu'll greet aifter.'*

> *'If Candlemas Day is fair an' clear*
> *Hid'll be twa winters that year.'*

On Candlemas 'flesh-maet' and rich brose or soup were substituted for the usual vegetarian diet. Beltane was observed chiefly as a term day, but the airt of wind and the weather on that day were regarded as predictive of the quality of the growing crop.

'If the wind is sooth,
There'll be bread for every mooth'
If the wind is east,
There'll be hunger for man an' baste;
If the wind is west,
The crop'll be lang an' slushy;
If the wind is nort',
The crop'll be short an' trig.'

John's Mass was celebrated in June by the lighting of large bonfires in the different districts. In Firth the three most important bonfires were: one above Moan, one in Kingsdale, and another above the shore near the boundary between Firth and Rendall. The superstitious element was strongly evidenced in rites performed round the John's Mass bonfire. Herd-boys and lasses too availed themselves of every opportunity to pull large quantities of heather, which were piled up in readiness for the day. When evening came the fire was lit by a live coal from a neighbouring house. A bone was always thrown into the fire whenever one could be readily got. The farmers who wished a bountiful crop the ensuing harvest, had large heathery torches made, lit them at the John's Mass fire, and never allowed them to get extinguished till the whole circumference of the fields had been traversed. This ceremony was gone through with the utmost gravity, after a solemn procession had circled round the blazing pile for some time. The two fires in the north side of Firth could be easily seen by those taking part in each, and probably two miles apart. At a certain previously arranged hour, a party from each fire set out with several heather torches, one of which was lit at each fire and carried along hurriedly till both parties met. This successfully accomplished meant that the farming interests of the two communities would meet with prosperity. As the dusky hour of midnight drew near, merriment waxed fierce and furious. After dancing till the early dawn set in, the young people wound up by jumping through the flames in a manner resembling the orgies of our Pagan ancestors, and by wildly pursuing each other home with blazing firebrands.

Hallowe'en, that night when witches and warlocks paced abroad, and special opportunity was given to those who wished 'to pierce the shades of dim futurity,' was celebrated in Orkney by many of the observances described by Burns in his 'Hallowe'en.' Kail-runts, pulled at random in the dark, symbolised the stature and build of one's future spouse, while the buds on the stalk intimated the number of one's progeny. In casting glasses, a glass was filled with water, and upon the white of an egg being poured into it, any one gifted with a fertile imagination could portray all the details of one's future.

Then the process which the national bard calls 'winnan three wechts o' naething' was very popular among young people. This was done by going out into the dark barn, leaving both doors open, and preforming a sham process of winnowing, having nought on the sieve but a pair of scissors or a knife. An apparition having the appearance of one's life partner was expected to pass the barn door. Another custom was to throw a ball of worsted down into the kiln, retaining the end of the worsted in the hand, and standing in the kiln-door, to unwind the ball, meanwhile repeating: 'Wha hauds i' me clrew's end?' In confirmation of the verity of these practices, it was told that a young woman winding her clew at the kiln door was replied to by the voice of the herd-boy. Incensed at not hearing the manly tones expected, she struck out in the dark. In after years, when cropping her husband's hair, she remarked on the 'norrows' (bumps) on his head. His explanation was: 'Du's thoo no mind the whack thoo gaed me i' the kiln-door on Hallowe'en?' A servant-girl after winnowing between the mill doors, to her disappointment saw no one pass but the master of the house, who, she understood, was just returning from a journey. On going into the house and remarking to the mistress that her man had arrived home, the woman, knowing that her husband had not yet come back, and suspecting what the girl had been about, said in humble submission: 'Be guid tae me bairns.' In a short time the woman died, and the girl was asked to take the place of step-mother.

Reminiscences of an Orkney Parish (1920)

ECHOES OF HOGMANAY

JOHN GOAR

(John Goar farmed at Galilee in Sanday, and when he retired, moved to Toab. He played the fiddle, and knew many old songs of shipwrecks, and as a result was in great demand when an Orkney Folk Club got under way. This poem of his captures the seasonal spirit perfectly.)

"This Hogmanay," says Jock tae Tam, "I think it would be wiser
Tae stay at home and hae wur dram, and shun the breathalyser.
Fur noo we must obey the law if wur tae stay alive
They plainly tell us ane an a' we mustna drink an drive."
Although we never left the place wae'd visitors galore
We sometimes even met a face wae'd never seen afore
They cam frae East, they cam frae West, fae all aroond they cam
Tae wish us luck an a' the best an hae a peedie dram.
They talked a lot on politics but mostly on the weather:
"The man abune, he's played such tricks it's floored us altogether.
It's rained fur days withoot a miss, sic gales an a'," said Tam.
'There's never been a year like this since Jeemsie lost his ram.
The barley and the tattie crop were just wan endless toil
Another year I'm giving up an gaan tae North Sea Oil."
Auld Jeannie says "If that's yer news, me ferm'll need us null.
Ah'll still keep on me twa-three coos, an buy a Char'lais bull
Ah'm sure twa'd be nae loss ava, fur if by chance he dees
Ah'll cut him up, his heid an a', an chuck him in the freeze."
"Furget it a'," auld Jeemsie says, "Wur in anither year
We'll dance an hope fur better days, so gaes yin fiddle here!"
Auld Jeannie cries "The very thing!" an took the floor wae ease:
"Ah'm sure a spot o' Highland fling will soople up me knees."
We then had mince an tatties, though I dinna want tae brag
But Ah'm sure that hid an tatties wid never turn the bag.

The auld clock chimed the warning; 'It's five o' clock,' she said;
It was far into the morning afore we got tae bed.
Afore I beat a fast retreat I've wan thing here tae say
I hope we'll a' be spared tae meet

anither Hogmanay!

BBC Radio Orkney recording

WINE, WOMEN & SONG

MARGARET HEADLEY

(Margaret Headley comes from Stronsay, where her parents, the Stevenson family, farmed at The Bu. She wrote stories for her own children, and then continued to write from enjoyment, her stories appearing first in issues of The Orcadian and then in the book The Voldro's Nest. She says that characters such as the Peedie Sandlo and the Groolie Belkie, and of course the Muckle Grullyan, have some of their roots in childhood stories and adventures, by the loch and sea shore. Their world is a gentle and happy one.)

'My Chove!' thought the Muckle Grullyan to himself as he burst in through his front door in a flurry of wind and hail, 'the Winter is surely come.'

He leaned heavily against the door to shut it upon the wind, and lowered the sneck. The fire was quite low, but he soon raked out the warm ashes and threw a pile of dry peats on the embers, and by the time he'd got his boots off and made his supper of blatho and oatmeal, the flames were roaring up the lum.

He hauled the old straw-backed stool into the blaze and sat down with *The Orcadian* and his mug of blatho. After he had read the fatstock prices and the latest news of the oil situation, there did not seem to by anything else of much importance, and he glanced idly over the SWRI reports.

Surely the institutes got up to some odd, not to say useless, occupations. Here were the women of Stenwick vying with one another on making the best use of half a roll of baler twine, while the Kirkhill ladies were busily making quilted golf-club covers. He was about to cast the newspaper scornfully aside when the words 'Wine Making' seemed to spring out of

the column before his eyes.

The ladies of the North Isles, if you please, were making wine! Now there was a useful occupation. Seemingly there was more to the North Isles ladies than berets and baltics.

He read on, eagerly, but the guarded references to demijohns and fermentation locks left him very little the wiser. He took a half-hearted gulp at his mug of blatho. It certainly did not do much to warm the cockles. Now, if he'd just had a bottle or two of home-made wine on hand... and why not, he decided. There was that old ale kirn up in the loft, and countless numbers of bottles, including one of P. C. Flett's, with the spring clip cork that might easily turn out to be a valuable antique one of these days. Surely, if a lot of daft women could make wine, he could make a vintage, par excellence.

An urgent visit to the public library resulted in a mass of information on wine-making, and on the way home, laden with equipment from the chemist, the Muckle Grullyan's mind was in a ferment, so to speak, with thoughts of must and elderflowers and foil caps and hydrometers.

Rather than going to the expense of buying glass demijohns, he decided to render the old ale kirn completely airtight, and make do with that. In any case, consider what an immense quantity it would contain, and forbye, wasn't that what they did in France?

After days of mashing and straining and the adding of yeast and pectic enzymes, a great barrel of elderberry wine, still slightly fermenting, was siphoned off and securely bound down, and left in the coolest part of the back porch.

The first two months went by easily, and by the time the wine had been re-siphoned back into the barrel, it was beginning to taste quite delicious; and when at the end of another three months it was ready for bottling, the Muckle Grullyan lifted the lid off the kirn with some eagerness.

The wine had indeed improved amazingly, and while he sorted out his bottle and corks, he kept sampling just a little and just a little more, till he began to feel somewhat drowsy, and decided to have a lie-down before he started the task of bottling.

As was to be expected, the Muckle Grullyan's activities had not gone unnoticed by his near neighbours, the Peedie Buckies, and when they found that the wine was about to be bottled they realised that their last chance of getting any was fading fast, for they'd never be able to broach a bottle.

Then it was discovered that the Muckle Grullyan had gone to sleep, with his wine all ready siphoned off. It was the work of a second to uncork the end of the siphon, and a stream of wine spread out across the floor and ran down the back step.

The Peedie Buckies were beside themselves with delight, swallowing down great mouthfuls of stuff until they became quite merry, not to say intoxicated. Someone began to sing, and fairly soon a noisy party was in progress.

After a time, the Muckle Grullyan became aware of the singing outside. A spirited rendering of 'Nellie Dean' was followed by an even more vigorous performance of 'Clementine,' and the Muckle Grullyan was on the point of joining in on the third verse with a particularly fine piece of harmony, when a dreadful suspicion began to form in his mind. He sprang unsteadily to his feet and, cramming on his facey kep, he blundered out into the porch.

A sight of unsurpassed debauchery met his eyes. A crowd of Peedie Buckies whirled and sang in a great pool of wine, which was gradually seeping away among the chingle.

As the Muckle Grullyan gazed in horror upon the sight, one of the Peedie Buckies who had drunk even more than the others, stepped unsteadily up to the Muckle Grullyan and addressed him carefully, if somewhat irreverently: 'I say, ossifer, where's your balloon? We'll blow it up and you can join the party.'

It was the final blow. His beautiful wine, all gone, and then to be mistaken for a policeman!

Almost enough to drive a body to drink!

The Voldro's Nest (1986)

HOGMANAY AND NEW YEAR

GEORGE MACKAY BROWN

(With contributors like Bob Johnston with his Stenwick stories and Spike cartoons, Ernest Marwick and Countrywoman with weekly columns, and Cubbie Roo's ba' reports, The Orkney Herald had a truly remarkable array of talented contributors. To top it all, its reporter who wrote under the pen-name of 'Islandman' was none other than George Mackay Brown. The reports do not always have a byline, but can readily be recognised; not surprisingly, each one is a little gem.)

After a week of dry frost, in which it seemed that conditions would be almost ideal for first-footing, the last few hours of 1950 saw torrential rain and a strong southerly wind, which lasted well after midnight. The sanguine hopes of the revellers were considerably dampened.

On the stroke of midnight, however, in spite of the torrential rain, there was a brilliant display of signal rockets from NLS *Pole Star* and the lifeboat station, which lasted for nearly a quarter of an hour. The show was seen from many parts of the South Isles and the West Mainland.

The fact that Hogmanay fell over a Sunday ensured that it was quieter than usual. Both places of seasonal 'good cheer,' the public bar and the British Legion Club, were closed.

But the entry of 1951, and incidentally the second half of the 20th century, rain-accompanied though it was, saw Stromness folk indulging in the usual celebrations.

First-footing is an ambitious affair nowadays. You not only visit your neighbours and friends, armed with the ritual bottle; your new year duty seems to be to discover how much of the town you can cover before dawn breaks. That at least seems to be the present tendency.

Many houses all over the town are lit up all night. Sounds of singing and merriment – and other sounds not quite so pleasant, such as 'bokking' in sinks – made the night a memorable one. The rain laid off about 1.30 am and thereafter first-footing was much brisker. When at last the first dawn of 1951 broke over Orphir, many a brave soul was still trekking from door to door on his New Year pilgrimage, game to the very last.

January the first was, generally speaking, a day of thick heads, parched palates and coated tongues. Thus inauspiciously each year begins in Stromness, and the citizens would be horrified to think of it beginning in any other way.

The Ness district of the town maintained its reputation, gained only a few years since, of being the brightest spot in town during the Hogmanay period. It was painted bright scarlet all over.

In the parish, all was quiet for the twelve hours following the birth of the new year. But first-footing went with a swing that afternoon and evening.

Strange to say, though celebrations were livelier than usual, there are no outstandingly macabre incidents to report.

We dare say that, next day, most Stromness men were glad they didn't have any Ba' to play, like their Kirkwall contemporaries.

The Orkney Herald, January 9th 1951

CHRISTMAS IN WARTIME

MARJORIE LINKLATER

(Of all the many ways in which Orkney has benefited from having produced a writer like Eric Linklater, not the least is through his marriage. Marjorie Linklater came to settle in Orkney after his death, and in the subsequent years has enriched Orkney life immensely, through her commitment to the arts and conservation and in fact to the whole Orkney way of life. She has been a pillar of St Magnus Festival, co-founder of the Traditional Folk Festival, frontline campaigner against uranium prospecting – to take just three examples. Her flair and sparkle would in one bygone age would have adorned the Renaissance court of James IV. Also, of course, she has resilience and humour in adversity, as the following demonstrates.)

By the beginning of June 1940, we in Orkney knew what it was like to 'be at war.' The first enemy bomb had fallen on the Bay of Eyreland, reducing a croft house to ruins. It was across the road from the place known as 'The Golden Slipper' which had a fairly lurid reputation, and for all we knew may have been aimed at it, but if so we could have done without German bombers acting as the wrath of God! (The owner was the first civilian casualty of the War.) Gun-sites and searchlights were strategically placed throughout the archipelago, but most were concentrated.around Scapa Flow.

In mid-June – when Orcadians were about to celebrate the longest day, midsummer – a terse military directive was issued to all personnel on duty in Orkney. "We have been warned that Germany is planning an invasion of Scapa Flow, by air, at midsummer. All wives and children of personnel serving in the armed forces are advised to vacate Orkney as soon as possible."

Eric, my husband, as a Captain in the Royal Engineers, was on the island of Flotta. They were responsible for the searchlights in the Flow – a vital part of our defence.

I shall never forget that (almost) midsummer night. Our home was Merkister in Dounby, and the great joy of June was the flowering of wild lupins all around. They thrived on uncultivated land – of which we had an acre or two on the shores of the Harray Loch – which were transformed in June to sheets of intense lilac, deep blue and pink.

The military directive, according to Eric, applied to all personnel in the armed forces. A passionate dialog followed between us on a perfect June night. "You must go," he said. "The two girls and my mother (living next door) will go with you to our friends in Aberdeen until the crisis is over."

"But the order applies only to families 'fae Sooth'," I said, "not to indigenous Orcadians." He brushed that aside. "You must think of me. How could I carry out my duties if I thought that you were being raped by the enemy?" Well, I hadn't thought of it that way, so I meekly gave in.

All the same I was angry and resentful. (My mother-in-law, I must mention, had circled the globe with her mother and father, a Captain in the Merchant Navy – mostly in sailing ships. She, remembering vital directives, wrapped her valuables – jewellery and such like – in chamois-leather bags and sewed them to her corsets!)

We spent a week or two in Aberdeen. The threat of invasion had spread throughout Scotland. Able-bodied Scots had armed themselves with pitch-forks to repel invaders, and were tearing down roadsign posts; but – nothing happened.

I could have returned to Orkney with Eric's mother, but I was so enraged by the banishment that I vowed I'd not go meekly back to the nest.

One of my sisters whose husband in the Royal Marines was in Ceylon suggested that we join forces and go for a summer holiday to Arran. Her two children – a boy and a girl – were joined by my oldest sister whose children – both boys – were a few years older. It was a joyous holiday although already shops were short of supplies.

Letters from Orkney were stern commands to return immediately. But the wife of the Marine and I had discovered through friends in the Borders that a very suitable house close to Newton St. Boswells was available for rent.

All this leads to Christmas 1940.

As it happened, the Argyll and Sutherland Highlanders were undergoing training in the vicinity. So we celebrated Christmas with chosen friends from the regiment – including an officer and his wife who were lodging with us. Not a 'gathering' but one or two were invited for Christmas dinner.

Everything was rationed, of course. So Christmas pudding with substitute sweetener and a modicum of dried fruit (dried egg and carefully collected margarine, flour etc.) did not taste quite as expected. Even the roast fowl turned out to be ancient and tough! Nor can I recall the accompanying wine. Very likely it was blackcurrant juice with whatever our guests could supply in the way of alcohol. But curiously, it remains in memory as an especially happy occasion.

Through that Christmas period, my sister and I did our best, along with other ladies in the vicinity, to entertain the troops. Most of us were amateurs but one or two were professionals. My sister had trained with Ninette de Valois as a ballet-dancer, and I suppose I could claim to have trained for the stage at RADA in London (Royal Academy of Dramatic Art); and a friend of ours really was a professional tapdancer – a regular performer with her partner in the Glasgow music halls.

It was exhilarating to perform, singing or dancing, before a packed male audience – always enthusiastic applause and, I've no doubt, some hilarious imitations when they returned to barracks!

When the regiment departed, bound for the East, little did we (or they) know that they were doomed. Captured almost immediately after landing in Singapore, they were set to work by the Japanese on the Chinese/Burma railway construction; only a few survived.

Finally I condescended to return to Orkney with the children and discovered, to my chagrin, that our tenants, an army doctor and his wife, had looked after Merkister perfectly, and, more annoying still, Eric had enjoyed along with all the troops defending Scapa Flow, the visits to Lyness in Hoy of leading stars from the London music-halls: Vera Lynn, Gracie Fields, and others whose names are now forgotten.

From being a vital War-Centre, Orkney, thanks to the evacuation by the Navy of Scapa Flow, had become a haven for deprived citizens. Not that the War Office had decided to withdraw all Fighting Personnel – far from it. A Balloon Barrage to protect the Flow had brought RAF reinforcements to Hoy, many of them Women's Corps. Hatston, Naval HQ for Air-Defence, was enlivened by trim WRENS. And where you get a concentration of de-orientated armed forces you get a spate of amusements; parties, stage-performances etc. which were greatly appreciated by local wives and families!

September 1995

WILLICK AND THE CHRISTMAS REPAST

DAVID SINCLAIR

(When the sociologists of some future age look back at North Sea oil in Orkney, the name of Willick o' Pirliebraes is likely to appear. If they take him for a historical figure and study his every word, it would be no more than appropriate, as from the start Willick has looked quite capable of coming off the printed page to sort out Islands Councillors, oilmen, contractors and anyone else requiring attention. He came into existence when David Sinclair, who runs Flotta's post office and shop, wanted to highlight the island's problems with a letter to The Orcadian, but found that it was getting too long, so – 'Having always been a short story addict and a lifelong admirer of the late Bob Johnston, who peopled the fictitious parish of Stenwick with such believable characters, I attempted to rewrite my letter in a short story format.' The rest, as they say, is history.)

It was Christmas afternoon, and everyone glancing in through the window of Pirliebraes' kitchen would have observed what appeared to be a typical Yuletide scene. The man of the house was dozing by the fireside, while his wife was engaged in preparing a duck for the oven. The mantelpiece and dresser were bedecked with greetings cards and, on the silent television set in a corner of the room, pop singers strutted their stuff on the Christmas edition of 'Top of the Pops.'

The man at the fireside stirred, and opened his eyes. Noticing this, his wife said, "Turn up the soond o' the TV, will thoo. Me hanns are aell grease aff o' this duck."

"Yin pop bruck's jist a daefance in the hoose. Whit are thoo wantin hid turned up for?" the man asked.

"Becase the Queen's Christmas speech'll be on in a meenit," his wife replied.

"Christmas," Willick o' Pirliebraes snarled. "Ah'm seeck o' hid, an the seuner hid's deun an by wae the better Ah'll be plaised."

"Oh, stop thee girnin, beuy," Maggie snapped. "This is Christmas day, a time o' goodwill an good cheer, bit aell thoo're done fae thoo got oot o' bed this mornin is moan aboot first wan thing an than anither."

"Weel, hid's little winder," Willick retorted. "Although this is Setterday, hid's jist lik a Sunday. Thir's no wark tae deu, thir's no milk or papers tae git fae Lairdy's shop, thir's nothin on the telly bit owld pictures that wir seen Best kens hoo offen afore, an the morn's Sunday again."

"Go back tae sleep, than," Maggie said. She forced the last of the oatmeal stuffing into the duck, covered its breast with bacon rashers and put the bird in the roasting tin.

"Ah'm no gaan back tae sleep, becase if I sleep any more the day, Ah'll no be able tae sleep whin I go tae bed the night."

"Hid's hard tae say whin thoo'll git tae bed the night, bacase thoo hiz a dance tae play at, mind on."

"That's right," Willick agreed. "Hid's fine teu that the Community Association keeps up the owld island tradition o' hivvin a dance on Christmas night. Ah'll better tak doon the fiddle an run ower twathree tunes tae git me fingars soopled up. Hid's a while noo fae the Rotten Gutter Band's hin an engagement."

"An hid'll be a while afore they hiv anither een, I warran," Maggie said scathingly. "The younger generation's no interested in lissenin tae an owld codger lik thee saain awey on a fiddle. The only raeson the Rotten Gutter Band's been asked tae play at this dance is becase thir's no right band wid come tae Flotta on a Christmas night."

"An hoo dis thoo ken whit's a right band an whit's a wrong een, tell me? Hoo well versed in music are thoo, an whit instrument dis thoo play?" Willick asked.

"Thoo kens bonny fine that I kinna play anything, bit I deu ken good music whin I hear hid."

"Aye, an I ken good maet whin hid's set doon in front o' me, bit that disna mean that I ken hoo tae cook hid."

Maggie sniffed, and said, "Weel, thoo're gaan tae hiv tae deu a grain o' cookin the day."

"Whit wey hid?"

"Becase efter I pit this duck in the oven, Ah'm gaan doon tae me mither wae her Christmas present, so if thoo wants thee denner the night, thoo'll hiv tae keep the fire on, an tak a look in the oven occasionally."

"My Mighty," Willick exclaimed, sitting bolt upright. "I kinna deu yin. Cookin's a woman's job."

"Weel, the night hid's gaan tae be a man's job," Maggie stated. "Unless, of coorse, thoo wants tinned maet for thee Christmas denner. If thoo're no gaan tae attend tae the cookin o' the duck, Ah'll jist hiv tae open a tin o' bully beef."

"Dirt tae thee bully beef," Willick said, getting to his feet. "Ah'm gaan for a walk up tae Stanger Head."

"Turn up the soond o' the TV afore thoo goes, please," Maggie said sweetly, and added in more severe tones, "An be back here aboot five o' clock tae keep an eye on the duck. Aell thoo his tae deu is keep pittin paets on the fire, an spoon some fat ower the burd noo an again."

At ten past five Willick arrived back at Pirliebraes. He sauntered into the kitchen, hoping to find Maggie bustling about there, but the only sound in the room was the snoring of the old collie dog who was stretched out in front of the black range.

"Dash hid aell, whar's yin wife gotten tae?" Willick muttered to himself. He put a couple of peats on the fire, gave it a quick poke, and opened the oven door. His mouth watered as the smell of roast duck wafted out. He looked around for the cloth that he had seen Maggie use to lift hot dishes out of the oven, and seeing no sign of it, grabbed the first thing that came to hand. This happened to be the overall which Maggie had discarded before going to visit her mother.

Using it as oven cloth, he lifted out the roasting tin and was about to set it on top of the range when a vehicle stopped outside the house. As he turned to look out of the window, the roasting tin slipped from his hands and hot fat cascaded across the top of the range. Some ran down over the firebars and ignited, sending flames shooting up to the mantelpiece. The old dog, rudely awakened when boiling fat dripped onto his backside, gave a yelp and hobbled out through the kitchen door as fast as his arthritic legs would carry him.

"Merry Christmas, one and all," a voice called, and Davick o' Lairdy, the island's shopkeeper, breezed into the room.

"Here, beuy, git a bucket o' watter as quick as thoo can," Willick shouted. "This confounded duck's set me hoose on fire."

"Right, let's get rid of the culprit," Davick said, picking up a mat from the floor. He threw it over the roasting tin, effectively smothering the flames on top of the range, and ran out of the kitchen with the roasting tin enveloped in the mat.

While Davick was gone, Willick thrashed the remaining flames into submission with Maggie's overall. Apart from a few scorch marks on the mantelpiece, a large burn on the mat on front of the fire, and a couple of incinerated Christmas cards, no great harm had been done.

"Beuy, that wis a close thing." Willick said, when Davick came back in. "I right near lost me Christmas denner."

"Your Christmas dinner," Davick said incredulously, "What about your house?"

"Ach, me hoose is insured," Willick replied. "Bit me denner's no."

"I see," Davick nodded. He was an old classmate of Willick's and, perhaps better than anyone else on the island, understood his friend's thought processes. "Right, let's get down to the reason for my unannounced visit this afternoon."

"Aye, I ken bonny fine that thoo're no here withoot an errant."

"I've come here to do you a favour."

"Oh, aye."

"Yes, I'm here to put money in your pocket."

"Huh," Willick grunted.

"Don't be so cynical," Davick grinned. "Let me get to the point. How many dozen hens' eggs can you sell me?"

"Are thoo tryin tae be funny? Whit the mischief are thoo wantin hen's eggs for on a Christmas night?"

"I'll come clean with you. The caterers down at the oil camp have run out of eggs and, as all their Mainland suppliers are closed for Christmas, they've asked me to try and get them a few dozen for the breakfasts tomorrow. So how many can you let me have?"

"Hing on a meenit, beuy. Spikkin o' poultry, whar's me duck?"

Davick shrugged. "I tossed your duck, roasting tin, et cetera, onto the lawn."

"Mighty me," Willick howled, and dashed out of the kitchen.

"Funny fellow," Davick said, shaking his head.

Shortly after, Willick returned and shook his fist in Davick's face. "Thoo gappis," he roared, "Thoo're done me oot o' me denner."

"I didn't do you out of your dinner. It was on fire, remember?"

"Git oot o' here," Willick raged. "Git oot o' here this meenit, thoo – , thoo vandal."

"What's the matter with you? Who are you calling a vandal? I've just saved your house from burning down around your ears."

"Mibbe that, bit thoo're deun me oot o' me denner."

"Your duck'll still be out on the lawn, if you really want what's left of it."

"Hid's no oot there at aell, becase in the time thoo held me bletherin here, the owld dog's made aff wae hid."

"He can't have eaten the duck. It would've been far too hot."

"Whin I gaed oot there, he wis makkin doon the road wae hid in his mooth. An if thoo his any wit, thoo'll better mak for doon the road teu, afore I brak oot on thee."

"I can see that in your present frame of mind it's impossible to reason with you, and I suppose that in the circumstances, it's only to be expected that you would be traumatised, but what about the eggs you were going to sell me?"

"I hiv dizzens o' eggs oot in the porch, bit thoo'll be the last een I wid sell them tae," Willick shouted, almost dancing with rage. "Jist clear oot o' here afore I lay hanns on thee."

"Okay, I'm going," Davick said, holding up his own hands in a token of surrender. He backed out through the kitchen door, and added, "If you change your mind about selling me those eggs, though, just give me a ring on the phone."

"Ah'm more likley tae gae thee a ringer on the lug for deuin me oot o' me denner," Willick threatened. He gazed at the fire-damage to his dwelling and muttered, "Beuy, beuy, this is been some oncairry."

When Maggie arrived home an hour later, she found Willick sitting at the fireside, dressed in his best suit. Although his freshly scrubbed face wore a benign expression, he was impatiently drumming his fingers on the arm of the chair.

"Whit's yin smell o' burnin?" she asked. "I hope hid's no wir duck."

"Hid's definitly no wir duck," Willick replied, getting to his feet.

"My stars!" Maggie exclaimed. "Whit's happened tae wir mantelpiece? Hid looks as if hid's been on fire."

"Thir wis a smaell mishap whin thoo wis oot," Willick said nonchalantly, and he proceeded to give his wife a graphic account of the conflagration.

"An wis Davick hurt?" Maggie asked when he had finished.

"Whit wae wis he tae be hurt?"

"Efter he haeved the rug ower the roastin tin. Thoo said hid wis jist a smaell bit o' blaze at first, bit whin he haeved the rug at the roastin tin, the flames gaed laeppin tae the reuff."

"He wisna hurt ataell, bit he wid hiv been if he'd stayed here any longer efter gaein wir denner tae the dog."

"Oh, weel, hid's a mercy nobody wis hurt," Maggie said, and began to take off her coat. "So noo I doot hid'll hiv tae be bully beef for wir Christmas denner efter aell."

"Dinna tak aff thee coat," Willick ordered. "Wir gaan oot for wir denner."

"Whar are wae tae go? Me mither'll hiv no maet tae spare, for shae's jist hivvin yin peerie cocky-chicken I took oot o' the freezer twa days ago."

"Wir gaan tae the Hilton for wir denner," Willick said smugly. The Flotta Hilton was the local name for the Elf Residential Building, where the oil workers had their meals.

Maggie looked aghast. "Wae kinna go there. Hid's only fock whar wirks for Elf that can git fed there."

"Wir gaan there for wir denner aell right, an Ah'll tell thee why. Davick wis up here tryin tae cadge eggs tae sell tae the Hilton, bit seein he near set the hoose on fire I widna gae him any. Efter he wis awey, though, I phoned the Hilton and telled them they could hiv as many eggs as they wanted if they gaed hiz wir Christmas denner there."

"An whit did they say?"

"They said thir wis no problem. If I took doon ten dizzen eggs wae me, wae wis welcome tae a mael there. Hid's gaan tae be turkey wae aell the trimmins, whitiver hid means, an plum puddin, an the manager said he might even gae hiz a dram afore wae go home. So instead o' stannin there wae thee mooth hingin open, jist button up thee coat again an wae'll git crackin. Ah'm fairly gaan tae enjoy me denner, bit no half as muckle as Ah'll enjoy seein Davick's face whin I tell him hoo I got hid." Willick grinned hugely at the thought of the two treats in store for him. He snatched his cap off the nail on the back of the kitchen door, and said, "Hurry up, pirrin, for hid's no ivery night that I tak thee oot tae a denner an than tae a dance efterwirds."

Orkney Talking Newspaper (December 1994)

BALLAD HUNTING IN THE ORKNEY ISLANDS

OTTO ANDERSSON

(When you hear the ballad of The Great Selkie of Sule Skerry sung by Joan Baez, you may not know that it was only a very unusual series of chain of events that saved the tune for her and for the rest of us. The story involves David Sinclair's uncle in Flotta, the Work family of Craigiefield, and the visit to Orkney in 1938 of the Finnish musicologist, Professor Otto Andersson, travelling with his wife in search of any possible traces of old Norse folk tunes.)

We arrived in Kirkwall on Saturday afternoon and, of course, immediately decided to attend the service in St Magnus the following Sunday. It is hard to describe one's impressions on approaching this wonderful structure, impressions which become still deeper when one enters the church. One's emotional response in St Magnus is in some way more intense than in other cathedrals. Can this be due to its great age or to the many historical memories and associations linked with it? Or is it one's consciousness of its insular situation, the overpowering fact that such a building should have been erected on an out-of-the way island? The reasons are no doubt many and varied.

When visiting churches abroad I often contacted the organists for information on musical and organological questions. Here I had an interesting talk with this organist and representative of church music in the Orkneys. I was surprised to hear that he was not a professional musician but a lawyer; nevertheless he presided at the organ with outstanding ability.

During my talk with the organist of St Magnus on this unforgettable Sunday the minister of the church, the Rev. G.

A. Fryer approached me, shook hands and bade me welcome
to Orkney; he had noticed visitors from abroad at his service
and was interested to know our business. As he heard that I
had travelled all the way from Finland to the Orkneys to collect
old ballads and folklore he asked me to have tea in his home.
He would like to introduce me, he said, to the most able local
expert in my field, Dr Hugh Marwick, the Director of
Education in Orkney. Dr Marwick could certainly give me
all the information I wanted for my work during the coming
week, he added.

I went to the house of the Rev. Fryer in the afternoon
with high expectations. I was received in a very generous way
by Mr and Mrs Fryer. The guests were friends of the family,
all distinguished Orcadians, and they were interested in the
traveller from afar who wished to inquire into the old ballad
tradition. Everyone knew that ballads had been common in
former days, and that both verses and music had been plentiful.
But no one believed that anything of importance had survived.
Dr Marwick gave a very disappointing account of the present
situation. It was definitely too late to collect ballads and ballad
tunes; the old Orkney tradition was dead, he said. And he
assured me that it was so, for during his tours of inspection of
the schools he had seen the decay of the old tradition. None
the less, Dr Marwick was ready to give me all possible assistance.
He promised to be at my disposal on the following Thursday
to take me around the Mainland.

Thus my first experiences were hardly encouraging. But
on the other hand this was nothing but the common tale that
folk songs had died out – a tale I knew so well. To a great
extent of course it is true. Nevertheless it has been repeatedly
shown that valuable records of old traditions can be noted
down in rural corners despite contrary local opinions. Nor
did I allow myself to be discouraged. I went on the assumption
that some musical traditions must still be alive in these remote
islands; and be that as it may I promised myself to do my best.

On the following day I started early in the morning using
my old method: I introduced myself to people indoors and
outdoors. The desk clerk in the Kirkwall hotel, guests in the

bar and workers on the quay were asked whether they used to sing traditional ballads or play old fiddle tunes themselves, or whether they knew anybody else who was supposed to do so. I told them that I was a Finlander interested in noting down the poetical and musical traditions of Orkney. It was something peculiar and unexpected that a man from Finland should visit these islands only to collect old ballads and fiddle music.

Therefore everyone listened with eagerness and was willing to help. By such inquiries I got one address here and another there and was able to pick up several singers and instrument-alists.

On Tuesday morning a man in the hotel, from whom I had made inquiries, pointed out a house on the seashore a mile or so from Kirkwall. 'Look,' he said, 'there at Craigiefield lives an old sailor, Captain Andrew Work; he certainly remembers old songs, at least some sea shanties; do pay a visit to him.' I followed the instructions and had a pleasant walk along the east side of the bay. Balfour Castle was to be seen in the distance on Shapinsay. On the right side was the beautiful landscape, treeless like all the Orkney Islands but dressed in fresh green.

Captain Work lived in a fairly comfortable villa. I entered, introduced myself and explained the aim of my visit. I was cordially received by Mr Work and his wife. Over a cup of tea we talked about old traditions and old songs. My host and hostess could easily make out what I was driving at and soon became interested in the subject. Unfortunately they had forgotten most of the songs they formerly used to sing and Mr Work was also weak after an illness. However, he granted my request and sang some songs, and so did Mrs Work.

Besides having personally given me some contributions for my collection, Captain Work also gave me most valuable information concerning ballad singing, which, however, I was able to make use of only to a small extent. He said there had been a housemaid from Flotta in his house one month earlier. she had told him that a famous old ballad singer, a Mr Sinclair, lived on that out-of-the-way island on the other side of Scapa Flow. Mr Work thought it worthwhile for me to pay him a visit. I studied the map upon my return to the hotel and found that a journey to Flotta was a great undertaking. It could only be done by motorboat from Stromness, the second town in the Orkneys on the West Mainland. But I was determined to go. An expedition was arranged for the following day through the clerk in the hotel.

We left Kirkwall early in the morning on the bus for Stromness. It was my first tour into the West Mainland and therefore thrilling in every way. The weather was not very fair, but clear enough to get a pleasant view over the landscape. We passed the village of Finstown and drove through a valley, where the visitor passes a nice plantation of trees, the only trees I observed in the country.

The view from Stromness is fascinating. Here the visitor sees the highest island in all the Orkneys, the mighty ridge of Hoy, opposite the Hoy Sound, which connects the Atlantic Ocean with Scapa Flow. Some small islands and the silhouette of Flotta are visible in the far distance to the South East.

We easily discovered the chartered motor-boat in the harbour. It was a biggish boat with a crew of two men, with a rowing-boat in tow. This was necessary, for Scapa Flow was not at its prettiest that day and the small boat was useful for landing at Flotta. We went past Hoy with its pleasant farmhouses below the hills, past the salvage vessels working on the sunken warships, past the small islands Cava and Fara, and so after an hour and a half we reached the harbour of Flotta, where we anchored. Since there was no pier to be found, we were forced to go ashore in the rowing-boat. A group of men had gathered on the beach and looked with curiosity to see what strangers were visiting their island. I tried immediately to get my bearings from some of them, but without success.

We walked towards the village together with the crowd. I had a conversation with several of the people in order to get advice, but no one knew of any ballad-singer on the isle. They did not know Mr Sinclair either. Probably the schoolmaster would be able to give some information, they said, when we approached the schoolhouse. I took the chance and entered.

We were greeted most cordially. The schoolmaster was surprised and pleased by our visit. He appreciated my efforts to discover old folk songs, but he was sorry to be unable to give me any help. There might by some old people living in a farmhouse close by, he said, but he was afraid they did not remember any songs. That proved correct when I visited this very primitive house; the people in it did not sing a single tune.

Finally the schoolmaster happened to remember a Mr Sinclair far over the hills in the east of the island. But he was not an old man and he lived in the opposite direction to that in which the old Mr Sinclair was supposed to live. Although it was uncertain whether a contact with the younger Sinclair would be of any use, I decided to go; I did not like to make the journey in vain and was therefore ready to examine every possibility.

My wife was shown by the schoolmaster into a comfortable room where she could wait until my return, while I got a stout-hearted little lad to show me the nearest way over fields and meadows. On the way we passed a farmhouse where we met a couple of men standing outside. I introduced myself and told them that I was visiting Flotta to collect old folk songs and was now on the way to a Mr Sinclair. Probably some of them used to sing, I cautiously suggested. Well, they answered, they might remember a tune or two, but it was now seed-time and therefore they were busy at work: one of the farmers had the seed-basket in his hand and was afraid of losing a precious sowing-day, while another was in a hurry with job at home. Finally one of them, Mr Joseph Simpson, broke off his work and took me into his home, where he sang several tunes.

Mr Simpson informed me that one of his old relatives had a large stock of tunes, but unfortunately I had no time left over for a visit. We continued our walk towards Mr Sinclair's farm, still directed by the lad: sometimes along a primitive road, sometimes straight on over the fields, up and down-hill; at long last we reached Mr Sinclair's farmhouse at the top of a hill. Fortunately we were greeted by the farmer himself, a good-looking fellow then about fifty. To begin with he denied being a ballad singer, and he did not know the other old person of his name that I asked about. We conversed for a while, whereafter he was ready to sing some songs since I had travelled such a long way to listen to him.

The second song later revealed itself as the tune to the 'Great Selkie of the Sule Skerrie.' I had no idea at the time that I was the first to write down the tune to this famous ballad. Its pure pentatonic form and the beautiful melodic line with its charming rhythm in irregular time, which gave the text a natural rendering, showed me that it was a very ancient tune I had set on paper. And the content of the only stanza Mr Sinclair was able to recollect proved that the ballad itself must be very remarkable.

'I am a man upon the land,
I am a Selchie in the sea.
And when I'm far from every strand,
My dwelling is in Solskerrie.'

Mr Sinclair did not remember any more songs, he said. He might, to be sure, possibly have recollected some if I had been able to stay longer with him. But the time for our return was fast approaching, and the distance to the harbour – via the schoolhouse – was considerable. Therefore I had to take leave of the kind singer and walk back with my young companion.

The crew was waiting on the beach. We boarded our motor-boat in the presence of a crowd of onlookers gathered to say goodbye. The return became quite adventurous. The weather had changed for the worse: hard head-wind and rain. In Hoy Sound the crossing became rough. The fierce tide was against us. The towing-line had broken in the heavy sea, and our rowing-boat was left drifting. However, we reached the harbour of Stromness safely, but too late for the bus; a taxi took us to Kirkwall Hotel late in the night.

Budkavlen (1954)

DANCING IN FLOTTA

DR TOM FLETT

(Dr Tom Flett was a lecturer in mathematics at Liverpool University, and with his wife wrote the standard book on traditional Scottish dancing. The following is one of a series of articles that he wrote for The Orkney Herald in the 1960s.)

The island of Flotta is unique in my experience. There, until about 1890, the islanders knew only one dance, the Orkney Sixsome Reel. I found this very surprising at first, but all the older people or, the island confirmed it. One elderly lady recalled a wedding held in her own home, at which there were about twenty couples present. The only dancing space available was a room about 12 feet by 15 feet, and there they danced six at a time, the fiddler sitting in one corner. When all had had their turn, the first set began all over again.

There was in fact no hall in Flotta at that time, so that the islanders had to dance in their own homes, where, as in the case of the wedding mentioned above, only six people could dance at one time. The restricted repertory becomes much more understandable when we realise that dancing only took place three or four times a year, and that even then one danced only one dance out of every seven or so.

This simple state of affairs ended in 1890 or 1891 when a dancing teacher from Inverness, Mr Smith, visited the island. The house of Windbreak was then being built, and was complete save for the internal dividing walls; and Mr Smith was able to obtain the use of this. Part of the floor was of wood, and part was of stone, but this was a minor detail. He stayed only for a fortnight, but held classes every evening except on Sundays. In the twelve evenings which were available to him, he taught the Foursome Reel, and Reel of Tulloch, Lancers, Quadrilles, Petronella, Flowers of Edinburgh, Triumph, Rory O'More, Haymakers, Highland Schottische, Waltz, Dutch Polka and the Ninepins Reel. It must have been a very intensive fortnight!

Before he left, Mr Smith sold some copies of a little ballroom guide which he had written, and, after he had left, the young men and girls met on the grass by the Bu', and learnt further from the dances from this (the Cumberland Reel was one such dance). There was such a craze for dancing that the lads would even practice the step for running the reel when following the plough.

Until the advent of Mr Smith, dances on Flotta had been leisurely affairs, with plenty of time between dances, and the fiddler was not over-worked. At the New Year's Dance after Mr Smith came, all this was changed, and the fiddler was so overworked that he wore the skin off the fingers of his left hand fingering the strings.

In spite of Mr Smith and the dances which he brought with him, the Sixsome Reel survived in Flotta until about 1910. Up until then it was invariably danced as 'The Bride's Reel' at a wedding. This was the first dance at a wedding, and was performed by the bride and groom, the best man and the bridesmaid, and the 'honest folk' (the last a married couple, usually related to the bride). These six danced the Sixsome Reel once over. The fiddler then paused for a few seconds, while the men (or sometimes the ladies) changed places so that the best man now danced with the bride, and the reel was repeated. Then the dancers again changed places so that the honest man now danced with the bride, and the reel was repeated for a third time.

I also met the usage of the Sixsome Reel as the Bride's Reel in South Ronaldshay. In all other places which I visited, however, I met no one who remembered the honest folk taking part in a wedding, and the Bride's Reel, the first dance at the wedding was a Foursome Reel, and was performed by the bride and groom, best man and bridesmaid.

After Mr Smith left Flotta, other dances were brought in

by some of the islanders themselves, including a Threesome Reel danced with handkerchiefs (I have met this from Aberdeenshire to the Borders), and the kissing dance Babbity Bowster (under the name of the 'Swine's Reel'). The First World War brought hundreds of troops to Flotta, and a dance programme of about 1920, kindly presented to me by Mr William Sutherland of Aval, lists a large number of couple dances from the south which presumably had been brought in by the troops, the Maxina, Boston-two-step, Winking Polka, French Minuet, Hesitation Waltz, Eva Three-Step and so on. Nevertheless, we still find the old Sixsome Reel appearing on the programme, and the last dance was still the Swine's Reel. The Sixsome Reel was in fact revived in Flotta for a short period round about 1920, but again fell into disuse.

I was not able to visit any of the North Isles, but I learnt a great deal about dancing in North Ronaldshay from Mr and Mrs Roy Scott, now living in Rendall. North Ronaldshay has one dance, a superb Eightsome Reel, which does not seem to be known elsewhere in Orkney. It is one of the most interesting of all Scottish folk dances.

The Sixsome Reel was also performed on North Ronaldshay, though it has not been performed there for some time now. It was not used as the Bride's Reel, however, this being the Foursome Reel. A teacher, Mr MacKenzie, taught dancing there a good many years ago, and the repertory was then much the same as in the islands which I visited.

I have already written enough to show that, so far as dancing is concerned, Orkney has a distinct tradition of its own. This tradition actually lies midway between the Highland and the Shetland traditions.

In all three places, Orkney, Shetland and the Highlands, the principal dances until comparatively recent times were reels. In Shetland, the commonest dance was a Sixsome Reel very similar to the Orkney Sixsome. And just as in Flotta and South Ronaldshay, the Sixsome Reel was used in Shetland as the Bride's Reel, the honest folk making the third couple. On the other hand, the Shetland Reel is in reel tempo only, while the Orkney Sixsome Reel is danced to both strathspey and reel, as are the reels belonging to the Highlands.

In the style of dancing, too, the Orkney reels followed those of the Highlands. Fairly elaborate setting steps were used (though on the whole simpler than those found in the Highlands), and the men at least raised their arms, snapped their fingers, and 'heuched.'

Orkney Herald

MARRIED IN ROUSAY

MAGGIE ANN CLOUSTON

(Mrs Maggie Ann Clouston was for quite a few years Orkney's oldest inhabitant, living to the age of 109. She was born at Claybank in Rousay in 1880 into a large family, in which everyone had to work from a young age, and all her life she enjoyed being active. Visiting her to record a interview when she was over 100 was a special pleasure. She would sit you down and make a cup of tea and cut a large slice of her birthday cake, and then gladly recall bygone days with great delight and good humour. This is part of a recording made on her 104th birthday with Kathryn Gourlay for Radio Orkney.)

I was nineteen when I married and he was twelve years older than me – old men's the best! Never marry a fisherman – it's a hard life when they're at the sea and coarse weather comes and peedie boats: very, very worrying. Waiting for them all the time and hearing they're coming in on a very coarse day and hauling their boat to a better piece and you hear them coming and you're glad to see them.

He was not a very strong man, he didn't last a long while – consumption was rife in those days but they can master it now. It was enormous, the number of folk that had consumption, and I was at the houses with it and I said I'm surely immune from it for I never took it, working so much among it, you see.

He went out every day; every morning he rose with the tide. When the tide was in they had to get up and go to sea, and they were small boats. We sold some of the fish and dried them on the dykes and pressed them, and we sold them in Kirkwall. Salted fish – the merchant bought them and sold them out of Kirkwall. Lobsters were very cheap in my young days. Lobsters were only a shilling, and they got eleven pence sometimes. That was the way we were kept down, you see. We could dress ourselves and go to the kirk too, all the same.

We had a set of clothes we kept aside and only put on on a Sunday for going to the kirk. What a grand day we had – everybody was walking then. There were no cars or anything; everybody was walking. What a grand time we had on the road, all speaking together! Fourteen miles was the size of Rousay right round it, and I've been round it on a Sunday, every bit of it and at my auntie's home at night for tea and milking the kye then. We'd go home at eight o'clock, running pieces of the road to get home on time then as well as now. Far better – dances at night, and all. And it was spoken about for a while. Now they never speak about a dance, it's just that common.

My father was the only fiddler on Rousay for a great while, and he taught the other ones to play. He was a grand fiddler; he just fairly fitted into the dances and the time. Polkas and Schottisches and the Four-Couple Reel and the Flowers of Edinburgh. There were dances that came in and they learnt them from Kirkwall: Rory O' More and Strip the Willow and the Queen Victoria.

We had a grand walk at our wedding, everybody went out with their partners and my father was there with the fiddle playing and played the whole road home and we were going with him – I suppose we did maybe fully two miles. We married in the house, decorated up for it. Plenty of whisky and plenty of ale and plenty of cakes and plum pudding and sweeties. We had our dance and we had our walk – the Quadrilles and the Lancers – that's dancing! – and they take the sweep and everybody takes hands and they sweep in and that's good dancing!

BBC Radio Orkney (May 17th 1984)

ORKNEY WEDDINGS

WALTER TRAILL DENNISON

(To Walter Traill Dennison goes the credit for having, in the words of Ernest Marwick, 'saved from extinction, single-handed, a whole corpus of myth, legend, and historical tradition which the educated Orcadians of his time ignored, even deplored,' and he did it with style and flair and warm-heartedness. He lived in Sanday from 1825 to 1894, where the Dennisons held the land of West Brough. Here his account of a typical Orkney wedding reaches the stage where the young people have begun dancing in the barn, while in the house their elders are for the time being story-telling, toasting and drinking.)

When the effects of the ale began to tell on the company a general move was made for the barn, where was organised what was called the 'Auld Folk's Dance.' This was composed of the very oldest men and women of the company, whose feeble hobbling added to the general merriment. Some eight people might be seen, bordering on fourscore, moving their bodies up and down to keep time with the music, while unable to move one foot before the other – each old man sometimes taking his venerable partner into his arms and giving her a hearty smack. The dancing of all parties was executed in what would now be considered a rude fashion – arms and hands being used as much as the feet, and loud exclamations of hilarity and encouragement ever and anon proceeding from the men.

The figures used in dancing were generally 'Reels.' There were the 'twasome,' that was the two-couple reel; the 'treesome,' the three-couple reel; and the 'aichtsome,' the four-couple reel. They also danced what was called the 'Cotillion,' but as the writer never saw it danced he is unable to say if it be the same as the French dance of that name. The finest figure of all their dances was what they called the 'Contra Dance,' which was a modification of the country dance. The dance which formed the finale will be described in its place.

The musical instruments during the last century were the violin or bagpipe, but formerly it was only a simple 'pipe,' which seems to have been a hybrid between the whistle and the flute. Dancing was generally continued until the seven stars were in the south-west – the stars being the nocturnal clock of our ancestors – when the company returned to the house for supper, where eating was resumed with renewed vigour; indeed, the quantities of food consumed at these feasts were almost incredible. But it must be remembered that the people were a strong, hard-working race, who rarely tasted butchers' meat except on holidays and at weddings.

At supper large quantities of pancakes (here called scones) were handed about on weichts. The scones were of various kinds. There were sowan-scones, alie-scones, garie-scones, and white-sides. The singing, story-telling and toasts were renewed at supper time. One thing that afforded great amusement was the singing of what were called 'here-meed rhymes.' These were rude ballads, composed by natives generally, celebrating some very melancholy, or else some extremely ludicrous event. These productions were only retained in the memory of the reciter.

After supper, dancing was resumed in the barn. Sometime in the early morning preparations were made for the 'Bride's Cog.' This contained a mixture of hot ale, gin, brandy, or whisky, with some eggs. From the mixture of the ardent spirits which this drink contained few of those whom the previous drinking had left sober were able to imbibe much of it without being intoxicated. There was also dropped into the large cog some pancakes, and in the cog was a long-handled spoon by which each party, if he chose, could help himself to a pancake, which was thoroughly soaked with the liquor.

The bride first drank from the cog, which was then passed to every person, and was replenished with warm liquor when required, till all were satisfied. It was not considered polite to ask for more drink after the bride's cog had passed round.

Great amusement was often created by secretly introducing something incongruous into this cog. It is related of one who fished up from the bottom of the cog with the long spoon something which he took for a pancake. After gnawing away at it for some time, he swore that this was the toughest morsel he had ever come across, for never till this moment had his teeth refused to chew what he put in his mouth. The article he was gnawing at turned out to be a large worsted mitten. Of course he must have been what the Scotch called 'blind foo.'

The next great event was putting the bride to bed. While the bride's cog was circulating, the bride stole away to her room, which for that time was generally in the chamber. She was attended by some of the strongest women of the party, not only for the purpose of helping her to undress, but for securing her clothes from the attacks of the young men, it being considered a great affront on the women and an honour to the men if the latter could succeed in running away with any part of the bride's dress. So eager were the men to obtain this that I have heard instances of one or two of them concealing themselves in the apartment for some time before the bride went to bed. By stratagem or force, it generally happened that the men got access to the room, when a dreadful scuffle immediately ensued between the males and females for possession of some part of the clothes.

I may here relate what was told me by a gentleman who took part in one of these scuffles. While some of his associates were struggling with the women for possession of a stocking, he managed to secure the bride's plaid, and, hiding it under his coat, rushed out of the house, followed by three of the strongest women of the party, who continued in hot pursuit for upwards of half a mile, where two of the pursuers came up with and laid violent hands on the delinquent, when a hard struggle ensued. The gentleman was considered one of the most powerful men in the country; after a long-continued struggle, the women succeeded in wresting the plaid from him and returning in triumph. I have heard of the stockings being pulled off the bride after she had gone to bed.

We must now return to the barn, where preparations were being made for the great and final dance. This, in one part of the country was called 'The Reel o' Barn,' and in other parts was called 'Bobadebouster.' When the piper strikes up the tune, one man dances in the middle of the floor alone for a minute or two. He then takes up his partner, and both dance, one of her hands in each of his. They then throw their arms over the head of another man. He dances between them; then, ducking his head under their arms, runs to and takes up his partner. He joins hands between the two first, thus enlarging the ring. The female in the centre next ducks, after dancing a little, and brings up a man, she going to the ring and he occupying the centre. Those in the ring, while this is going on, dance with circular motion, so that the whole party is always going round with the sun. The dance goes on till the last man in the room is in the centre. He then takes the place of the man who first began the dance, and after dancing a few minutes in the centre, brings his partner there, when he ducks under the arms of the ring and retires to his seat. The ring is thus gradually diminished until all the parties have danced out.

Care was always taken in this dance never to unlock the hands of those in the ring unless when receiving or parting with a dancer at the proper time. If the dancer in the centre happened to be a clumsy man or bashful girl, when attempting to get out under the arms of the ring, which was continually moving around, these parties were liable to be thrown down while passing the moving barrier; but such accidents only added to the general amusement.

At the close of this dance the revelries were generally ended for the first day. But, in old times, wedding festivities were often continued for three or four days together, and each morning found most of the guests inebriated. Indeed, wedding feasts seem at one time to have lasted as long as there was anything for the guests to eat and drink.

Marriage and Wedding Feasts in Orkney (1885)

WANTED: ONE RED FLAG

JOHN D. MACKAY

---

*(When John D. Mackay died in December 1970, The Orcadian
recorded that with his passing 'something unique and irreplaceable
has been taken from Orkney life,' and 25 years on that assessment
seems just as true. A native of Papa Westray, he taught in Stronsay,
Kirkwall, and North Ronaldsay before becoming Headmaster in
Sanday in 1946. His love of learning, and his brilliance in digesting
new ideas and introducing them into the community, ran through
everything he did, from his teaching and his evening classes, to his
letters to the local press. These letters were masterpieces, relished by
readers for their wonderfully elegant humour, but time and again
opening up issues that would otherwise have been allowed to wither.
He would write on world affairs, and he would write on the neglect of
the North Isles by those in authority. His life richly deserves a book,
and is shortly to receive it. In the meantime, here is a sample of the
master in full flow.)*

Sir – The news that Her Majesty the Queen has expressed
a desire at least to look at the North Isles is, indeed, most
gratifying. That she should even mention them makes one
wonder if, perhaps, some hint of our plight may not have
reached her ears where she sits among the ermine and gold of
Buckingham Palace.

During the last two or three years, we have been visited
by whole regiments of the Mandarin class from St Andrew's
House, and from Westminster. They have been, as Mandarins
usually are, most affable, telling us how wonderful we are, and
how admirable are all our efforts, but practically nothing has
happened as a result of their visits. The Hydro-Electric Board
has not supplied us with current so that a majority of us cannot

benefit from the extension of T.V. to the area: our transport services are as old-fashioned and as inadequate as ever: and we do not yet have a daily mail. When our roads get snow-bound, large enough vehicles cannot be found to drag the snow ploughs which the County Council give us to keep us quiet, or, perhaps, to show us what can be done in more advanced areas. Shortly, it will take less time to land on the Moon than what it takes to travel from Kirkwall to Westray.

Now, our British newspapers always assure us that such primitive conditions cannot exist in a great nation like ours. They assert that poor creatures who are denied the benefits of civilization are only to be found in the Union of Soviet Socialist Republics. As, of course, dear Editor, I have great faith in the British Press, I can only conclude that, somehow, the North Isles of Orkney must have been annexed by the Soviet Union when no one was looking, and when there were no Mandarins about.

Since this is so, would it not be an excellent plan to fly the Soviet flag from an elevated piece of ground in the North Isles when the Royal yacht passes our shores? I am certain that Her Majesty would notice such an unusual object. When told the reason for its presence, she might even consider that it might be expedient for her to stimulate slow-moving County Councillors, and forgetful Mandarins, from Above. They seem to be completely impervious to all the prods we can give them from Below.

Yours etc.
John D. Mackay

Letter to the Editor, The Orcadian, February 26th 1959

HARVEST

WILLIAM SMITH

———————————

(The local press have been well served over the years by their parish correspondents. William Smith, who contributed from Sandwick to The Orcadian at the turn of the century, typifies in these two excerpts the freshness of detail that went into so many local contributions.)

The season. The present time is an instance how farm work, more than any other industry, is dependent on weather conditions. For the past few days none has passed without rain some time or other. The greater proportion of the crop is still on the fields, in a bad condition. The sheaves are completely waterlogged, and grain is commencing to sprout. Very little can be done in the circumstances, unless to set up fallen sheaves, and keep all as upright as possible, which is a great advantage, thus allowing the rain to run off the sheaf. Some are shifting the stooks so as to save new grass, and also to have full advantage of drier weather, by a change of position. Had the season been spring instead of harvest, little fault would perhaps have been found with the situation. Some days are mild and warm with grass keeping green. The lark is still giving utterance to song, but the robin redbreast is coming about the houses, neither of which indicate settled weather at this time of the year.

Improvements. Each year implements reducing the output of manual labour are being introduced. Some self-binding reapers have been got this season on moderately-sized farms, and the owners speak in highest praise of the benefit. Alterations are also being made on threshing machinery. Already there are three threshing mills driven by oil engines in the parish, and it is said three more are to be put in this season.

THRASHING

JAMES OMOND

(A prized possession for an Orkney musician is an Omond fiddle. James Omond taught at the Kirbister School in Stromness parish, taking up fiddlemaking after his health gave way under the overcrowded conditions. His son, also James Omond, followed into teaching, and became Headmaster of Kirbister School in Orphir. A brilliant teacher, he wrote the standard book on Orkney bird recognition. His series in The Orcadian in 1911, looking at Orkney 80 life years before, later became a book.)

In winter the first job usually was thrashing in the barn with flails by the light of the cruizie or, in some cases, candles, and at the larger farm houses this work was finished before daylight. The sheaves were laid on a rounded threshing floor of hard packed clay, and the men, stripped to the waist, stood at each side wielding the flails with an alternate rhythmic stroke, knocking the oats off the straw. There was a door on each side of the barn opposite to each other, and the oats winnowed out of a kaisie (straw woven basket) or winnowing cubbie, in the draught caused by opening both the doors.

If the wind were strong and shelter was required for the heap of oats, the height of the draught was regulated by sticking up two pins, one at each side of the door, and winding simmons or straw ropes about them to the required height. Sometimes, when the weather was suitable, the winnowing was done outside on a 'flackie' or straw mat measuring about eight feet by four feet. It will be obeserved that straw was indispensable to the welfare of the Orkney farmer; indeed it was put to as many uses as the coconut palm is to the dweller in the desert.

The Orcadian (1911)

MANSIE'S THRESHING

ROBERT RENDALL

(Robert Rendall has aptly been described by George Mackay Brown as one of the outstsnding Orkneymen of the twentieth century, with a many-faceted mind that could span the arts and sciences in one imaginative field of vision. Born in 1898 of a Westray family, he became a draper to trade, in his spare time exploring the shore and the rock pools in his study of Orkney's shells, in which he became the acknowledged expert. He only began writing poetry when in his late 40s, being inspired by the classical writers of ancient Greece and Rome. After his death in 1967, his work gradually went out of print, but has now been republished with a biography thanks to the dedication and care of Neil Dickson from Kilmarnock. In the final selection, 'Mansie's Threshing' was omitted; so here it now is.)

The mune was up, and the starnie lift
Luk'd doun wi' an eeriesome licht,
As Mansie ap-raise fae his neuk-bed
In the wee sma 'oors o' the nicht.

Green O green grew the corn.

The Lady's Elwand was high in the aist
Wi' mony anither starn,
When Mansie ap-raise fae his neuk-bed,
And syne gaed through tae the barn.

Green O green grew the corn.

Lady's Elwand: belt of Orion.

He saa the mune-beams glint on the wa'
    Lik' spooks on kirk-yaird graves,
As doun fae the twart-backs he tuk' the flail
    Tae thresh oot his load o' shaeves.

    O bonnie and green grew the corn.

He grippid a shaef, he rissl'd the heid,
    He cuist it apae the floor.
"Trow tak me," he said, "if shaeves lik' this
    Were seen on the place afore."

    Green O green grew the corn.

"The neebors minted what nane wad neem
    When the knowe cam' under the pleugh;
But heth, the stooks were cairted heem,
    And biggid a denty skroo."

    Green O green grew the corn.

"Wha meddle wi' Pickie-knowes, said they,
    Ill-skaith wad them befa' –
But never a ferlie cam' near me,
    Nor ever a thing ava."

    O green grew the corn on the knowe.

The soople, swung abune his heid,
    Had twirled but three times three,
When Mansie afore him b' the wa'
    An aasome sight did see.

    Green O green grew the corn.

twart-backs: cross-beams.
minted: darkly hinted.
skroo: small stack.

A black-haired bockie, wi een that lowed
  Lik' the flame in a howkit neep,
A faersomlik' mooth wi' a yellow tooth,
  And lugs that hung in a fleep.

   O bonnie and green grew the corn.

It glowered and gloomed, till the haet haet
  bluid
  Louped fast in Mansie's veins,
For the bockie's flail, baith soople and staff,
  Wis a deid man's white shank-banes.

   O green on the knowe grew the corn.

Then up spak Mansie and stootly said,
  "A'm blide o' thee company,
But bees' thoo Pight, or barrow-wight,
  Come thresh fornent o' me."

   O bonnie and green grew the corn.

"For the baists maun be fed, and the windlins
  spread,
  Though the world be fu' o' spooks,
The corn be mill'd, and the girnel fill'd
  Wi' bere fae the guid corn-stooks."

   Green, green grew the corn on the knowe.

Aa' through the barn the mettins spret
  Lik' sparks fae a smiddy fire,
And aye the stour the thicker cam'
  And the haeps o' strae raise higher.

   Green O green grew the corn.
    fleep: loose fold.
    mettins: seeds of grain.
    spret: sprang up.

Faster and fiercer fell the flails,
  Till the mune cam' roond on the wa',
And the cruisie flickered, and gaed clean oot,
  And they heard the reid cock craa.

   Green O green grew the corn.

Hoo it befell, O none can tell,
  But when they brak doon the door,
Wi' build on his heid, they fand him deid
  On an empty threshing floor.

   O green grew the corn on the knowe.

They laid him in the green kirk-yaird,
  But for midnights three times three,
They heard deep doun in the hert o' the
  knowe
   The soond o' revelrie.

   Green O green grew the corn.

   "Green O green grew the corn,
   Bonnie and green grew the corn,
   Green on the knowe grew the corn – o
   Bonie and green grew the corn."

IN THE BUT-HOOSE

JAMES OMOND

The lum or opening in the roof for the smoke was about two feet square, and made of wood tied round with simmons outside, and was not placed over the fire, but three or four feet behind the back, and a board used for skylin was shifted to the wind side by a long pole fastened to it.

Having entered the kitchen we are saluted by peat reek, for, no matter how well the lum is skyled, clouds of smoke circle everywhere. We must step warily, as over the but door is the halan' or boards on which the hens sit, to our right are the calves, polly sheep and, even in some cases, the work ox tied to the gable. In front is the 'back' with, it may be, a week's ashes resting against it. We have heard it said that on one occasion a lad had climbed to the lum of a house to look down and see who were in, and, the boards giving away, he overbalanced and fell among the ashes behind the 'back' with such a thud that he sent the 'stoor' flying in all directions and nearly 'smoored' the folk. For convenience in removing the ashes from the fire, there was often a hole right through the back opposite to where the fire was set, so that when the big back peat was removed or burnt done, the ashes could be pushed through behind.

Having safely passed the livestock, there is on our left a flag bink to set pails on, and underneath it may be two or three geese sitting on eggs. A little care is required for a stranger to negotiate a passage clear of their long necks, and now we see the hale and hearty guidwife and hear her cheery 'Come in bye to the straw-backed stool,' and if it were not for the reek smarting in our eyes, we feel very comfortable before the roaring peat fire.

WER NEW BYRE

MINNIE RUSSELL

(Moving to more recent times, Minnie Russell's Orkney cheese was renowned when she was at Brecks and Myres in Shapinsay, before she and Hughie retired to Kirkwall. When the Irish firm who installed their new byre asked how it was doing, she told them in verse.)

Dear Masstock, we got your letter all right
So I'll sit down and write you an answer tonight
And tell you in language that's simple and clear
What we think o' the byre now we've had it five year.

Well, the stock that we keep on the farm is near double
And yet they are fed wi' just half o' the trouble,
The cattle are lookan their best for a while
And Hughie goes round wi' a beautiful smile.

The grass is as green as the Emerald Isle
The slurry is surely improving the soil;
Abundance of silage to put in the pit,
And barley all golden for feeding with it.

Even the wife no more has a face that is sour
For Hughie has now taken oot a door,
And there is a kitchen all shining and new
Where the old byre stood wi' the calf and the coo.

A dairy as weel for cheese and for butter
So she needno go oot in the weet and the gutter
So it's the Masstock System for Brecks and Myres
And that good fortune attend you is our earnest desire.

SAVING TIME IN SHAPINSAY

A. J. FIRTH

(We continue in Shapinsay, which is where Sandy Firth spent his early days. One of his great interests is the sea, and he has put much work into the development of Orkney sailing and the running of the Sea Cadets. Another great interest is Orkney's history, through its buildings and stories of community life. His teaching career was in both nautical and technical subjects, and in a highly active retirement he puts much energy and skill into the development of Orkney Wireless Museum and the work of Orkney Heritage Society.)

In World War I it was realised that industry, and power, could be saved by altering the clocks in Britain to one hour forward. This was not at all popular in farming communities, and in Shapinsay was referred to as 'German Time', and was generally ignored as there was very little contact with the outside world. At the end of hostilities things reverted to normal, and the episode was largely forgotten.

On Sunday, 3rd September 1939 (a flat calm day of pouring rain in Shapinsay), Britain again found herself at war, and it was not long before the Government remembered that both fuel and power would be saved if the country was to alter its clocks, by putting the time one hour forward, so as to gain daylight at the start to the working day. A law was passed, and on a certain Sunday morning, at 1am, the deed was done.

In Shapinsay the Kirk Session called a meeting, the NFU held a meeting, the School Management Committee held a meeting, and the District Council held a meeting. They could remember the trouble caused the last time, and were not happy.

This new law was all very well in Whitehall, but in Shapinsay people had been going to Kirk on a Sunday at the same time probably ever since the Reformation, and the beasts would not understand it if their feeding pattern were interrupted. It was decided that the Kirk would go in at 'God's Time' – i.e. one hour later than the official time. Here a problem arose as the Congregational Church did not mind the advantage of the time shift, and went 'modern.'

The NFU decided that it was going to mean a revolution in living patterns, but that everyone could do as they pleased. Some opted to follow Whitehall, and some to keep 'God's Time.'

At school there could not be any flexibility. The County Council followed the law, as did the Education Committee, and all schools had to conform. A member of the District Council was sent to lobby the teachers, but their hands were tied, and in any case there were a goodly number of scholars from the Congregational community.

The island had a few hundred service personnel from all three services, and they were on Government time. The drifter which ran back and fore for the Forces also had its clock set on Daylight Saving Time, to use the official title.

The local steamer, the SS *Iona* had to carry the mails, and take livestock in to the Mart, and groceries from wholesalers back to Shapinsay, so there could be no opting out there.

With mutterings about dire repercussions for meddling with things the way they always had been, the island settled down to endure the problems raised. The Post Office was opened according to a unique scheme in that the mail came and was delivered on DST, but the shop which went with the Post Office had to extend its day by an hour to accommodate those who had rebelled – trade must come first!

Some families changed their clocks, and some did not, and some had two clocks on the same mantelshelf, marked with both times! Remember that very, very few people had watches, and no one carried these valuable items round with them in those days. Out in the field, the sun gave an indication as to the time, and some horses were expert at when to stop, but the majority of folk relied on a towel at a window, a whistle, a bell or a bairn sent out to bring the workers in.

The next spring saw the dawn of utter chaos...

Whitehall decreed that as the scheme had been such a huge success the country would go one better and introduce – *BRITISH DOUBLE SUMMER TIME.*

Consider the consternation. All the previous year's problems were now completely compounded.

On the old time clocks, the SS *Iona* left Balfour Pier at 7 am; it then reached Kirkwall at 9.30. It left Kirkwall at 4 pm and reached Balfour Village at 2.30 pm.

Farm servants who had just started the last half yoke of the day would see friends from farms on BDST as it was called, washed, shaved, and in their flannels, heading off down to the RAF station at the village to enjoy a pint of beer, and a game of darts at the Canteen.

The schools were now two hours adrift from the old, or Island Time, and this led to quite a number of families moving over to BDST, or at least going half way.

Visitors to the island had to be very careful. There is the lovely story of LAC Jack Croft who was stationed at Netherbutton, and when their CO eventually got permission to allow the troops (Netherbutton had WAAF's) to travel outwith the Kirkwall/St Mary's restriction, he headed, with some pals, for Shapinsay as fast as their legs would carry them, to buy hens, eggs, butter and cheese to send home. (Every day hundreds of service personnel boarded the drifters which ran between Kirkwall and Balfour Village.)

They took so long to walk in to Kirkwall that it was the second drifter of the day they caught. This meant that there were a good few dozen customers scouring the island before they landed, and so they had to walk further up the island to get the stores they were looking for. They ended up in the Hollandstown area, and were rewarded with all that they needed, and asked in for a cup of tea forbye. They noticed the time, and were delighted to see that they still had time to take in the scenery, as they wended their way back to the pier. We all know what awaited them when they got there! 'Oh boys, boys, the last drifter left more than an hour ago.'

They had to be in camp before 'Lights Out' or face a serious charge. Theirs was a Top Secret job, and there were no excuses or reserves to stand in! Now, I did mention the R.AF.base at the pier; this was for the two Air Sea Rescue Launches which were based in the bay, and they had a tender.

Now it just happened that the CO had been invited over to HMS *Sparrowhawk* at Kirkwall, along with Captain Henson R.NR of the Naval Loop Minefield Base on the island, and before these officers were escorted down the steps, on to the tender for the half-hour run to Kirkwall, a group of very worried military personnel were smuggled on board, and had a very uncomfortable trip back to Kirkwall, stowed in the engine compartment of the tender. We are happy to know that not one of Jack's eggs was lost, and the entire consignment reached the 'Home Counties' in pristine condition.

For the farms who did comply to regulations there were other problems. Shapinsay had a huge hen population, and they had to be cooped up at night in case of vermin. Now free range hens don't know about clocks, and they objected strongly to being herded in for the night in the middle of the day! Another problem was that the dew was still heavy in the mornings, and a lot of work had to wait until it had lifted.

Lastly there were the social problems raised.

There was an 11pm curfew which lasted until 7am. Now this was no problem if a social evening was organised with all parties on the same time scale – but if a couple were courting...

In at least one case there was a newly married couple with the husband working at home with BDST, but they were living at his wife's farm, where they were on Old Time.' This meant that he came home after a hard day's work, ready to put his feet up, whilst she still had work to do, and she was ready for an evening's entertainment when he was ready for bed! In the mornings, her family were still due two hours' sleep when he was looking for his breakfast, or heading off to eat with his folks.

Time, they say, is the great healer, and the war ended, as did all this messing about with clocks – or did it?

October 1995

THE IONA

BILL DENNISON

(Bill and Sylvia Dennison's stories of life aboard the coaster Elwick Bay, where Bill was skipper and Sylvia cook, have brought them a legion of fans through radio broadcasts, television features, and two books of hilarious adventures. Their humour is beautifully crisp and laconic, but underneath it is a real feeling for the sea and ships, which comes out in accounts such as Bill's story of the Iona, the vessel with which the Dennison family served Shapinsay for so many years. The following two short extracts are taken from this; the original in its entirety is a classic piece of maritime and social history.)

The *Iona* was built to the orders of John Reid, who must have been an industrial tycoon in his day as a grain-merchant, fish curer, and ship-owner. Not being a man to waste energy, he married a widow, Mrs Hume, who had two brothers, John and David, both sailors, not to mention a spare daughter. That is where the Dennisons came in. My grandfather married the boss's daughter – always a good move, if you wish to rise in any Company.

Just below the north end of Balfour Village the beach is hard but not rocky, and that was where the *Iona* was built. There was not enough room to build her in the conventional way – stern to the sea; so they built her side-on. Three carpenters undertook this daunting task, no doubt assisted by spare labour from the fish-curing stations and grain stores.

In 1893 she was completed, turned round on greased timber and launched, or rather hauled into the sea, by men and horses. I have seen the vat in which my grandmother and great-grand mother made ale. It must have taken at least four brews to get the *Iona* launched. The horses in Shapinsay were heavy drinkers in those days.

The steam engine was bought from Thomas Reid & Sons of Paisley and carried up from the Clyde by another embryonic steamship, complete with boiler, donkey engine, and steam winch. It must have been quite a feat to set everything in place with two ships lying side by side at Balfour Pier, one heeling with the weight on her derrick and the other an empty hull rolling gently. I bet modern ship-builders could not do it.

Boilers have to be lagged to retain heat. I doubt if anybody in Shapinsay knew this until they read the instructions that came with the powdered asbestos. Asbestos has no inherent linear strength and should be laced with cotton, hemp or some fibre. This was no problem. There was plenty of straw at Balfour Mains, a 400-acre farm. In those days nobody had heard of asbestos poisoning, so nobody suffered, probably due to plenty of fresh air and my grandmother's home brew. Some of the elders of Orkney may have heard of free-range hens. In Shapinsay in 1893 there were no others. When the asbestos was mixed, twelve cart-loads of straw were waiting, the contents including a large number of eggs of varying age. The eggs were added to the asbestos mixture and the whole plastered into place with the straw. Once the eggs were cooked after the boiler was lit, the steel inside was irrelevant.

A couple of decades later, a portion of the boiler had to be exposed for Board of Trade survey. The boiler-maker hammered for hours with his cold-chisel without making a dent. Only when he erupted to complain, as boiler-makers will, did the truth emerge. The Iona's reputation took on enhanced prestige. Not even P&O or Cunard White Star lagged their boilers with a straw omelette.

The County Show was good for the Iona's business. Even as today, the islands had their own cattle shows first. The successful local farmers had to visit the East and West Mainland shows to size up the opposition and have a holiday. A few unfortunates were accompanied by their wives, but the *Iona* could always use the extra fares.

The big day started early. We had to load the precious beasts, discharge them carefully in Kirkwall, and be back in time for the 0930 sailing with passengers and mail. I do not know the breed of these cattle except for the fact that they were all black and did not speak French. Definitely not Charollais. I do remember that they were as glossy as the Duke of Wellington's boots when they were landed in Kirkwall. No doubt one was called Cherry and another Blossom, and the crew looked like stand-ins for the Black and White Minstrel show. When they were black and white.

By the time Shapinsay had been evacuated to Kirkwall, the cattle shows were over, so we took the whole lot back. The farmers who had won had full bottles, the less fortunate only a half. Celebration beats commiseration, and the Iona's crew were the only shoulders to lean on. Robbie Groat kept his boiler-room floor covered in red-hot ashes. My father had his own technique, not tongue in cheek, but in the neck of the bottle; two simulated gulps and you were home and dry. When the cows came home the Iona's crew were not only black, but minstrels as well. Fortunately my father knew the drill and had a reserve crew standing by, none over the age of eighteen.

They say it is tough at the top, but it was worse at the back end of the *Iona*. About 1800 there was a roisterous departure from Kirkwall. The Earls Thorfinn and Sigurd and the *Iona* all left at the same time. The cat-calls and by-names were shouted to and fro:

'Shapinsay sheep-baa, baa, baa! Stronsay Limpets! Westray Auks! Eday Skarfs! Rousay Mares! – and Sanday Gruellie belkies!'

There were other words as well, none complimentary. What fun there was, and the memories lasted for months. We did not even have to pay the BBC for a licence.

It was unfortunate for me that I was appointed Second Mate of the *Iona* one County Show afternoon. The grandiose title meant that I had to get out the stern-ropes. All the way from Kirkwall to Shapinsay I coiled and recoiled my heaving line; five fathoms of the best hemp with a large, intricate weighted knot called a 'monkey's fist' at the firing end.

We arrived at Balfour Pier at dead low water. Young Bobbie Groat up for'ard had it easy, but I was determined to do my best. After a couple of practice swings, I made a violent heave, and hit the President of the Shapinsay SWRI under her port ear-hole as she erupted from the cabin. Having been battered nigh unto death by heavyweight handbags at the age of thirteen, it is little wonder that I still can not throw heaving-lines after fifty-odd years at sea.

The Lammas Market was a more light-hearted affair, mostly women and children. The ship's certificate was for 71 passengers and we never carried more than 140. My father's instructions were to count the legs as they came down the gangway and divide by four.

'After all, we are mainly a cattle boat.'

To conclude my recollections of the passenger trade, I must mention John and Mary of a prosperous farm. It was not too long after World War Two and I was home on leave, sailing the *Iona* to give my father a break. About eleven o'clock, while driving the winch, I saw an agitated figure abreast the port rigging. I stopped and went over.

'Boy, Billy, don't wait if I'm late. I've a pound Mary does'na ken aboot.'

John had just sold a beast, but was not allowed to Kirkwall on his own. Somehow he had managed to slip his halter. At sailing time Mary came on board with the other passengers, and only when the gangway was removed did she notice the absence of John. There was a rattle of the wheelhouse door, not unexpected.

'John's nohere. Ye're no sailing withoot him!' As I was still in the Navy, I didn't have to hesitate with my answer.

'Madam, we are carrying His Majesty's Mail and sail to schedule!' For once I was not thumped by a handbag, possibly because I was framed by the wheelhouse door, and Mary didn't have the room to get in a good swing. John was recovered and returned on our afternoon sailing. He had spent his pound wisely and well, in fact I guess he'd had two pounds or many friends. His fate on return to home is not recorded, and I do not want an 'X' certificate on this story.

Bombay to Elwick Bay (1993)

A PAINTED SHIP

J. A. ROUSAY

(Jim Rousay is a graduate of Strathclyde University, where his teachers included Charles Palliser, author of The Quincunx, and he spent a year studying creative writing at Connecticut State University. He lives in his native town of Kirkwall, where he is custodian of St Magnus Cathedral. His studies have also included art and architecture, and his visual sense can be seen in the beautifully-painted image at the centre of the following story. What the ship is, and how the people around it live, gradually becomes apparent as the story proceeds.)

Either he had been named after the ship or the ship had been named after him.

He was not sure of this.

It was one of those fine things that his mother often told him. He would sit by her card table in the long gallery. She played a game she called 'O, alone, O,' or something like that.

Sometimes she would sing out the name of the game as she laid card upon card, breaking up her silly song to tell him, almost fiercely, of his father, the ship, his grandparents, and anything else he asked about.

He thought that she was very foolish when she threw back her head and gave out one of her high-pitched and short little laughs.

Then the cards would fairly *Thump!* on to the baize, and he knew then it was time to go out into the garden.

She remained in the gallery, where the pictures of his forebears hung.

'All dead,' said Peter the handy-man, who was really a big boy. He spent his time going between the house and the garden.

When Peter was in the house, he would sometimes carry him upstairs in his arms, or riding high on his shoulders. Then they would look at the pictures.

'All dead,' Peter would say, and then, as to himself, 'Thank God.'

Peter was very strong and was sixteen. He had fine golden hairs on his arms. It was like resting in a robust and warm high chair.

'All your great-grandfathers, sailing men all, all dead now,' bright-haired Peter would say to him, as he carried him up and down the length of the gallery on those afternoons he was in the house.

Sometimes Peter would play with him, and let him run his fingers over his face, tracing imaginary lines over his scattering of freckles and around his opening and closing blueish-grey eyes. He liked to tug at Peter's tightly curled ears, and, most of all, to run his fingers through the thicknesses of white-gold hair, over and back from the boy's forehead.

The would stop at each picture in turn. 'That's your great-uncle Carlos,' Peter would say, and for a minute or so, they would stand before the darkest of the dark portraits. 'He went down with his ship long before your father was born.'

Long-nosed and black-eyed, great-uncle Carlos frowned down on them, his eyes glinting like the shiny black peak of his captain's cap. In the background, they could just make out the shapes of a palm tree and a sailing ship.

'He was not a good man,' said Peter, and then they would move on, to more darkening formal portraits, and on to naive native efforts whose colours and shapes seemed all wrong, past yellowing barques and clippers sailing on impossible seas under greenish-blue skies, past great-grandmother Mauberly's carefully painted bowls of roses, until they came to the picture he liked the best of all, the picture of *his* ship, his namesake (*or was it the other way around?*), the good ship *Laurence T.*

She (*why was a boy's name she?*) was made in Canada (*Peter had said*), and she was really a fishing boat though she looked like a yacht, though much larger, that one of his southern cousins owned.

'She's a schooner,' Peter said, so he believed him, and listened dutifully while the boy pointed out the finely elongated spoon of her stern and the long curved sweep of her stem. The artist had done well, much better than some of the others, for the *Laurence T.* looked a living and moving ship, cutting like a dagger through the waves and spume of an ocean sea. Above the waves, her only background was a flying sky in which a solitary bird with black-tipped wings of enormous span skimmed the peaks of the waves. Taut as a bow, with all jibs and topsails set and full, the dark green ship made her passage.

'She'll be coming in soon,' said Peter. 'She sails as straight and as true as an arrow.'

Safe within the encircling warmth of the boy's arms, he thought the sea deadly cold, and feared delightfully for the safety of the ship.

A small and dark-haired boy, he lived in the great white stone house which was nearly two field-widths from the hamlet and the sea. He still retained a hint of babyhood plumpness, though he knew he'd soon be six.

The house, cool in the summers and cold during the winters, was large enough to become lost in. It possessed a plethora of cellars and attic rooms, and it was from the high and difficult windows of some of these latter that he tried the dim blue of the southern horizon with the heavy captain's glasses. Stood upon its end, it was almost as tall as himself. Hours would pass thus in one or the other of the two rooms; not even Peter, who seemed able to go anywhere in the house, intruded upon him here.

He watched the sky line until his eyes saw moving transparent worms against the blue, but the Chinese-plate stillness was broken by no sails other than the tan lugs of the local fishing skiffs in the way between the headland and the islet, making for the entrance channel to the bay and the hamlet.

Only the distant sounds of the tea things being set interrupted those solitary afternoons among the warm silences

and the dust motes. Then he would put the leather-bound
glass away for that day, ease the little window shut, and slip
back downstairs.

His mother was punctual where the routines of the house
were involved. They waited until a quick grace was said, his
mother leading. Then they would carefully eat, while the girl
from the village waited upon them. Peter ate separately in a
dim old shed at the bottom of the garden, close to the dank
north wall. He thought that Peter might have wanted to eat
with them in the house, though when he asked his mother,
she immediately said No! and he had dared not asked her
why. He remembered how she had reddened. Maybe she was
angry at the girl, who had suddenly taken a kind of coughing
fit as she leaned over him for the used dishes.

He was always glad to be away from the table, to remain
out in the ebbing afternoon light until the girl came looking
for him. He could barely understand her village speech, though
Peter's too had more than a little of the inflection. "But then,
I'm not purely of them," he would then mysteriously say, with
a wink of his left eye.

There was not warmth in the girl. She treated him like
part of the furniture, something which she had to work with,
to clean, maintain, and polish. Her black hair was straggly and
she smelled wrong.

He left it at that.

In his dreams the ship would come in.

He would see her coming around the sane spit's point at
the end of the grey afternoon, sleek and silent, her long green
hull slipping through the little pale waves of the haven, her
white sails now being furled, the faint squeaks of the blocks
entering into his dream songs and sounds. He'd meet her at
the quay, staying out of the way as the ropes were thrown,
caught, and their loops dropped over the white painted iron
bollards. Then the captain would spring her in closer to the
harbour and the ropes would stretch and shiver and throw off
sprays of water. The crew would swing over the heavy wicker
fenders which would protect the glossy green of the hull from

the stones of the quay, two men to each.

Then the gangplank would be rolled forward and lifted up, and he would take his first shaking steps on it, fearful of the dark and swelling water down there beneath his feet, between the sheer of the hull and the dark brown weed of the pier wall.

Yet his father would surely be there, to reach over from the other side and pick him up, to then swing him high and wide, out and over the golden wood of the ship's deck, while he screamed with delight and Mother and Peter looked on approvingly!

Sometimes, he imagined that the ship would come in the night, when he was sound asleep.

He knew that it would have to arrive on one of those nights when the late summer was edging towards Autumn, when the air was still warm and the lighthouse flashed against the thick dark dusk of the southern horizon.

Then, with lights muted and fitful, with moths birring and patterning against the yellow, red and green lantern glasses, it would appear out of the sea gloom, to nuzzle the quay softly with its dark hull. There would be no great shouting or cheering from either ship or shore in that midnight hour; there were only the lanterns to douse before sleep.

Then he'd wake up early on the bright morning, look out over a sea of glass and see her at the quay, glistening green hull and golden pine mainmast, and edged with pure white rails, all shimmering in the light and warmth of the morning sun.

Peter would have the dogcart ready by the time he had dressed and eaten, and the three of them would jingle along the track to the village, all on this bright and yellow day.

In the meantime, he imagined the voyages of the ship, remembering what Mother and Peter had told him of the long southward journey to a place called Guinea, where there was gold. Mother had shown him a golden guinea, and Peter had snorted, had said that it seemed to be the wrong colour as far as he was concerned, but Mother had flashed him a fierce look and he just laughed.

He knew that the ship then went on to another far place, Brazil, and then to the hot Indies, before coming back home to the quay. He imagined her slipping along in the tropic night, leaving a glowing wake, while the crew slept under the stars and the late watch sang soft songs to the captain, his father, to keep him awake at the helm. He could see his dark and handsome face by the dim glow of the binnacle lamp, and smell the tobacco smoke from his quiet pipe.

In the north, with the sea becoming greyer as she sailed on into the lowering winter light, the crew would bundle themselves against the growing cold and huddle around the foc'sle stove in their spare time. Then the hatches would be battened down, and tarpaulins placed to keep the cargo dry.

Here, he stopped and thought. What *did* the *Laurence T.* carry?

Once, he had asked Peter. Did the *Laurence T.* carry gold from Guinea, piles of ingots laid carefully in the hold? Or did she carry lions and brilliant birds? Peter looked at him oddly for a bit, and then said that the ship carried blackbirds, if it ever carried anything live. Then he went away, shaking his head and muttering.

It was strange to imagine a whole ship full of chortling and flying birds. But then blackbirds *had* been baked in pies, and in the village, the ship's chandler had one which he had taught to speak, after he had removed a bone from its throat, or so he said. The bird had never spoken to him though, but he now harboured a growing feeling that the breed was special in some obscure way.

After all, would a ship as special as the *Laurence T.* carry any old birds? He thought not.

Mother and Peter were walking down towards the end of the garden. Mother, taller than Peter, wore her pale green silk dress and the white bonnet which he knew had a bunch of tiny blue forget-me-not flowers, made of satin and wire, on its front. He had wanted to come with them, but both of them had said *No!* and then Peter promised he would take him out on the bay in the rowing gig soon, if he busied himself in the house.

He had gone to his attic room, which was cool and still on this grey afternoon. Only the greedy old spider in the corner of the window moved. He prodded at his tunnel of web with a bent and rusty nail, and watched it scuttle back and forth in the hope of catching a fly.

He was leaning out the window crooning to himself. His song was wordless, rising and falling as his mind wandered and willed it. The dull green flat lands surrounding the house were as featureless as the grey sky and the darker grey of the sea. His song rose and fell. Peter and Mother passed beneath him and did not look up. He murmured on, his eye idly following the flight of a solitary gull out to the mouth of the bay.

She slipped from behind the dark line of point, her presence breaking forever the stillness of the afternoon. Out of the corner of his eye he saw her, and turned, disbelieving, barely crediting what he knew he was seeing.

The ship, indifferently, drew well clear of the spit and set herself up for the final leg to the haven. He watched her topsails coming down as she tacked, watched as her hull grew larger and darker in the ambivalent light.

Then he regained his sense of expectancy and mission and ran yelling, a mad thing, down and down to where the people were.

Peter had the gig ready, and helped Mother up. He did not look pleased, and his face was nearly as red as the coachman's livery he had put on. He drove down the track too fast, while the *Laurence T.* came nearer.

Her sails were down now, and she was drifting slowly towards the quayside, her bare frame prodded along by a light air which had sprung up. Soon, he saw the ropes come snaking out, to be caught and attached. He could see the sailors and the shore men heaving her in close, and then they entered the hamlet and rattled over the few cobbles to the quay.

She was not the immaculate ship of his imagination, for her journeys had tired her. Great scores and scrapes ran the length of the green hull, while near to the bow, some of her planks had been stove in and roughly patched with sacking and unpainted deal. The name too had suffered, indeed was barely readable, its white paint long battered away by head seas. Her rails were bent and streaked with rust, her anchors hung out and askew, and long stains of nacreous blue and brown oxides descended from their hawse-pipes to her waterline; here he watched queasily as acres of green and hair-like weed streamed and floated as she rose and fell.

The gangplank was laid and secured and the crew, all local boys and men, trooped on down. One spat into the oily and dark water and spoke gruffly to his mate, who laughed raucously. Then they were gone. Many of them lived in the town, some ten miles inland from the hamlet, though some broke their journey immediately in the solitary ale house at the head of the pier. Those who remained on board did so because the ship was their home.

His father appeared, dressed for the shore. He wore a waistcoat of scrolled green on a canary-yellow base and high brown boots. Gold shone from the heavy watch chain which adorned his middle.

He was a tall, thin, and dark man, but now with many strands of grey showing in his sleek black hair. His face smiled down at him, but it had none of the softness he had expected it to have. Though his father stretched out his arms in welcome, Peter had to prod him forward towards them, while his mother scolded at his reluctance. The thin and high-boned face swung down as he carefully trod the gnarled and worn wood, trying not to look at the water below. Arms encircled him, arms smelling of mothballs, arms as strong as steel wires. He let them clasp, gave no sign of either submission or resistance. Stubble rasped on his cheek as the arms clutched him tighter; he wished for Peter's arms over and again, but Peter was standing at the other end of the plank with his mother. Then, it was all over and he found his feet on the rising and falling deck of the *Laurence T.*

Mother and Peter came on board, Peter walking close behind, ready to check her if she wavered in her step. He still looked uncomfortable, and perhaps a little frightened too. He remained his distance while the captain and his wife embraced, and drew apart, eyeing one another like duellists. What words passed between them went low and unheard.

The ship was his! It did not matter now if he was ignored, if his mother and father were looking angry at each other and at Peter, for this great green ship, home from the oceans and the ports of the world, its cargoes carried and delivered, was his to explore.

Amidships, a mahogany companionway door was half open. He sneaked over to it and disappeared, cat-like, down into the dark.

Peter had been sent to look for the boy.

'Damn him,' he muttered, and was then not sure is he had meant the captain or his misplaced son. *A reconciliation of sorts seemed to have been effected up on deck; he was now Peter the hand again, a mere boy to be ordered around, a forelock-tugger, a lackey. Yet everyone knew who his father was supposed to have been. It was his damned fair hair which consistently gave the lie though. Pity. But think on what he knew now! Not that they had ever, but it had been coming close, had not the damned ship arrived nearly a fortnight too soon. She had been as keen as himself, all that arm touching and smiling, "Oh, Peter, come and do this for me," and, "Peter, could you help me in the garden," and making some excuse and becoming all bossy again when she saw the effect of her interest on him. But it would have happened. Not for nothing did he keep the shed door locked. The brat would have run blabbing about the bed he had seen in there, and his plans would have been exposed, for she was nothing if not sharp. But where was the brat now?*

Then, he checked himself. *The boy trusted him.* He was not even envious of the boy, for he suspected that his life was stifled and lonely. He knew that she found him an encumbrance, and was always trying to fob him off on himself or one of the other servants. He supposed that when he came to be of a proper school age, the boy would be sent to one of those posh schools in the south.

Yet, envy in plenty was around. It was so unfair, if what his mother hinted at were true. Only he did not look as like him as the boy did, he was so fair. Oh yes, he was envious. Only he could not see the envy and the boy at the same time. He continued his search for the child.

He hated this ship. Bad it was having to be on her, up on deck in the fresh air, but never would he have stomached being below decks of his own volition. *But a servant he was, and servants generally do their master's bidding. He knew too much, that was his problem.*

As a lad, hanging around the pier with the other boys, he had once asked his mother why he and some few others had been warned not to play on board the *Laurence T.* when she lay in port. The answer had shocked him, for he had a child's balance in his conceptions of right and wrong in those days, long before he was taken on by the owner of the vessel and thus became a kind of accomplice in what he still saw as a dark wrong.

The boy was turning innocently with a set of leg irons when Peter found him. *'There are over a hundred of them,'* he said. *'What are they for, Peter?'*

They regarded one another. The half-light only served to heighten the foetid and sickly odours of the main hold. On either side of them stretched the dark lines of iron and chain. Peter wanted to tell him everything about this ship of the damned, this floating hypocrisy, this illegal black-runner, who year in and out, exchanged misery for gold on the Great Atlantic Triangle.

His mouth worked, unhappily.

'Perches,' he said, eventually. *'For the blackbirds.'*

January 1990

THE DRIFTWOOD FIDDLE

HARRY BERRY

(Harry Berry's storytelling skills led to television and radio appearances, including a Radio 4 Pick of the Year. He was a talented artist, with pictures of ships and stormy seas, an all-round musician, and contributed much to the community. Born in London early this century, he left home at the age of 15 to join the Navy, where he spent 26 years as a diver. He came to Orkney to work on salvage in Scapa Flow, and then as Customs Officer in Lyness. His great love of the sea, his warm affection for people, and his admiration of work well done all characterise this story.)

Across the stretch of heather that separated our houses I had watched him making a pile of the furniture in the little front garden, and somehow I knew that he was going to burn it. He was the only son, and had come north on the death of his mother. His visits would be brief, for he was now a busy man in London; and except for a simple memento or two, he would quickly dispose of the rest of the ancient furniture.

He saw me watching him, cupped his hands and called me across. We both stood before the large confused heap of household effects; old chairs, tables, sofas. He nodded towards the pile.

'I'm burning the lot – it's alive with woodworm!'

For a moment we stood silent, looking at the pile; it was surmounted by the old wooden bed on which he was born, intimate, standing in the garish light of day. Suddenly he said, turning, 'Oh yes, this old trunk, it's full of Dad's tools. I suppose Mother must have put all Dad's things in it after he died.'

He opened the creaking lid and went on, 'I remember you had a lot of fun using these tools when you first settled up here – just take anything you want and I'll burn the rest.'

I recognised the tools; I *had* used them in the old man's workshop twenty-five years before. In those days old Sam Dickson, besides being an able member of the lifeboat's crew, was a jobbing carpenter, but his hobby was building small boats into which he incorporated pieces of seasoned driftwood salvaged from the Pentland Firth shore which he combed frequently. I remember the day he picked up the piece of beautifully grained Balkan maple and how, he had told me, he would make a fiddle from it. Eventually he gave up his boatbuilding and devoted all his spare time to the making of his fiddle, and after six months of infinitely careful work it was completed.

I had seen it only the once, when it was finished. It hung above his bench, perfect. The lovely grain of the Balkan maple body, the slender neck of Cuban mahogany, cut from some choice piece of some wrecked ship's furniture, the scroll exquisitely carved, the ebony fingerboard that had once been some mariner's chart ruler – the driftwood fiddle.

We had admired it for a long time in silence, and I could see the old man was immensely proud of his work. Then, unhooking it from the piece of string from which it hung, he laid it against his shoulder as some crofter fiddlers are apt to hold this instrument, and played a reel or two.

I thought it sounded a little harsh, and somehow the old chap seemed to read my thoughts; for he said, very softly,

'I wonder how it would sound in the hands of a master.'

He re-hung it above the bench, and tomorrow he would give the already glass-like varnish its final burnish. But old Sam did not see another day – he died in his sleep that night.

Now I looked down into the chest holding the tools we had both used, badly rusted, with the wooden parts peppered by worm. I lifted them out one by one, laying them reverently in a pile beside the chest; then right on the bottom of the trunk I saw it – the case the old fellow had made to hold his masterpiece.

I gently lifted it out and laid it on the corner of the trunk; the iron snibs broke as I lifted them, the finely powdered dust floated down as I opened the lid, and there before my astonished eyes it lay, as perfect as the day I had last seen it – the driftwood fiddle. The steel strings had long since rusted away and the gut strings hung loose, but the fiddle was untouched, and the flames in the Balkan maple danced as I turned it over in the weak sunlight. For a long time I regarded it with incredulity, then was aware that young Dickson was watching me. I turned my head and our eyes met.

'You keep it,' he said.

If a visitor from the south should enter an Orkney croft where the fiddle is played, not unusually the instrument will be seen hanging against some part of the living-room wall and old Sam used to keep his old fiddle hanging in such a place; so it followed that I took down my best painting and gave the driftwood fiddle this place of honour in my own house. For almost two years it hung there, until I received a letter from an old acquaintance – a concert violinist of some repute, to say that he and a friend would be coming north for a day or two's fishing.

That late August evening is still vivid in my memory. We sat before the red, glowing peat fire in my rather large, lamplit drawing-room, and I told my visitors the story of the fiddle. I'd had the instrument re-strung and my piano tuned, and I asked the violinist to gratify the old man's wish – not that he would hear it, but that I could compare it, for I still remembered how it had sounded twenty-seven years before, harsh and strident; but now I would hear it in the hands of a master.

The elder man, the accompanist, sat at the piano looking through a pile of music for a suitable piece, while the violinist charged the bow with resin, tuned the strings precisely and ran swiftly over some scale. I saw the piece they had chosen was Panaini's Caprice in D Major. Then came the opening bars, the piano soft, the violin sweet, vibrant, alive and infinitely sad, filling the large room with its response to the master's touch.

And then I saw HIM!

Shadowy at first, over there against the softly lamplit wall beside the violinist; now he became gradually clearer until he stood plainly, exactly as I had known him, in his stained white apron, with his white hair, his hands clasped to his chest, his weathered brown face a study of dreamy wistfulness.

Only in some vague way was I aware of the music as it sped on, towards the tempestuous last movement, the violin living, singing, delivering itself of its very soul, the old man watching the fingers of the master as they flew over the keyboard of his creation. And then the last not. As it sadly died away, old Sam turned his head slowly and looked straight at me – smiled once – and was gone.

Until now I have never mentioned my experience to a soul, for after all, it may only have been a figment of my own imagination. Yet sometimes on a winter's night, when the room is bathed in the soft glow of the oil lamps, and the flames in the wood of the fiddle dance as they reflect back the flicker of a peat fire, I fall to wondering, in a whimsical kind of way, what it was that kept the woodworm from it during its dark twenty-five years – and even now, I notice, it never seems to collect the dust…

Collected in *The Driftwood Fiddle* (1990)

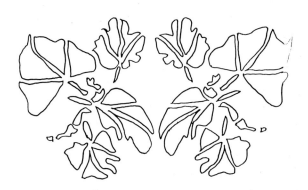

REQUIESCANT

WILLIAM GROUNDWATER

(As Rector of Stromness Academy William Groundwater was regarded
by his pupils with an immense respect and affection as someone with
a great natural authority and strength of character, and a warm sense
of humour. He studied and taught English literature, but he also had
a lifelong interest in natural history, writing the Nature Notes column
in The Orcadian for some time. His love of the natural world comes
out in this poem, published in Ernest Marwick's Anthology of Orkney
Verse; years later it was read at his funeral.)

Here when they crept to take their rest
Beside the Atlantic's ageless beat
Stray winds that wander down the west
And sifting sands about their feet
Soothed them at last, and stanched the flow
Of dreams they cherished long ago.

Beyond the call of wind or tide
Regrets are dead and yearnings spent;
She'll seek no more for smiles to hide
Her sweet sad disillusionment,
Nor he with spectral flagon toast,
Derisively, Ambition's ghost.

For them the lusty dawn no more
Will raise its multi-throated shout,
Nor tired waves creep home to shore
As one by one the stars come out;
Stubble and friendly grass entreat
No more the welcome of their feet.

From the hushed chamber where they lie
Will steal at last reluctantly,
Through rustling curtains of the sky,
The immortal sounds of earth and sea,
Constrained in other ears to ring
Their joy's phantasmal trumpeting.

And when the shades of evening fall
Beside the church, beneath the hill,
As earth's last dusk shall cover all
The frailties of the human will,
Asleep, forgetting, they shall twine,
The surge of the sea their anodyne.

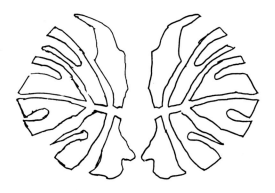

LAURA MEETS A
TRAVELLER

MARY BRUNTON

(Mary Brunton, born Mary Balfour in 1778 at the Bu in Burray, was descended on her mother's side from the great English military family of Ligoniers. She died young, but not before she had published two novels which influenced subsequent writers. In the first of these, highly admired by Jane Austen whose first published work appeared a year later, the heroine Laura Montreville has something of the calm maturity and delicious enjoyment of human variety that characterises Elizabeth Bennet in Pride and Prejudice. In this scene, Laura has travelled with her father from Scotland to London, where they take lodgings with a Mrs Dawkins who has two daughters. Julia, still unmarried, is a devotee of sentimental literature. Her more down-to-earth married sister Kate arrives with her husband, Mr Jones the haberdasher.)

As soon as the commotion occasioned by their entrance was over, and Laura formally made acquainted with the lady, Mrs Dawkins began, 'I hopes, Kate, you ha'nt forgot how to tell about your jaunt to Scotland; for this young lady staid tea just o'purpose to hear it.'

'Oh, that I ha'nt,' said Mrs Jones, 'I'm sure I shall remember it the longest day I have to live.'

'Pray Miss,' added she, turning to Laura, 'was you ever in Glasgow?'

'Never,' said Laura; 'but I have heard that it is a fine city.'

'Ay, but I've been there first and last eleven days; and I can say for it, it is really a handsome town, and a mort of good white-stone houses in it. For you see, when Mr Jones married me, he had not been altogether satisfied with his rider, and he thoft as he'd go down to Glasgow himself and do business;

and that he'd make it do for his wedding jaunt, and that would be killing two dogs with one stone.'

'That was certainly an excellent plan,' said Laura.

'Well,' continued Mrs Jones, 'when we'd been about a week in Glasgow, we were had to dine one day with Mr Mactavish, as supplies Mr Jones with ginghams; and he talked about some grand house of one of your Scotch dukes, and said as how we musn't go home without seeing it. So we thought since we had come so far, we might as well see what was to be seen.'

'Certainly,' said Laura, at the pause which was made to take breath, and receive approbation.

'Well, we went down along the river, which, to say truth, is very pretty, tho'f it be not turfed, nor kept neat round the edges, to a place they call Dumbarton; where there is a rock, for all the world, like an ill-made sugar loaf, with a slice oou o' the middle on't; and they told us there was a castle on it, but such a castle!'

'Pray, sister,' said Miss Julia, 'have you an accurate idea of what constitutes a castle? of the keeps, the turrets, the winding staircases, and the portcullis?'

'Bless you, my dear,' returned the traveller, 'ha'nt I seen Windsor Castle, and t'other's no more like it – no more than nothing at all. Howsoever, we slept that night at a very decent sort of an inn; and Mr Jones thought as we were so comfortable, we had best come back to sleep. So as the duke's house was but thirty miles off, we thought if we set off soon in the morning, we might get back at night. So off we set, and went two stages to breakfast, at a place with one of their outlandish names; and to be sartain, when we got there, we were as hungry as hounds. Well, we called for hot rolls; and, do but think, there wasn't no such thing to be had for love or money.'

Mrs Jones paused to give Laura time for the expression of pity; but she remained silent, and Mrs Jones resumed: 'Well they brought us a loaf as old as St Paul's, and some good enough butter; so thinks I, I'll make us some good warm toast; for I loves to make the best of a bad bargain. So I bid the waiter bring us the toast-stool; but if you had seen how he stared, –

why, the pore fellor had never heard of no such thing in his life. Then they shewed us a huge mountain, as black as a sootbag, just opposite the window, and said as we must go up there; but, thinks I, catch us at that; for if we be so bad off here for breakfast, what shall we be there for dinner. So my husband and I were of a mind upon it, to get back to Glasgow as fast as we could; for, though to be sure it cost us a power of money coming down, yet, thinks we, the first loss is the best.'

'What would I have given,' cried Miss Julia, turning up the whites of her eyes, 'to have been permitted to mingle my sighs with the mountain breezes!' Mrs Jones was accustomed to her sister's nonsense, and she only shrugged her shoulders. But Mrs Dawkins, provoked that her daughter should be so much more than usually ridiculous before a stranger, said, 'Why, child, how can you be so silly, – what in the world should you do sighing o' top of a Scotch hill? I dare to say, if you were there you might sigh long enough before you'd find such a comfortable cup of tea, as what you have in your hand.'

Miss Julia disdained reply; but turning to our heroine, she addressed her in a tone so amusingly sentimental, that Laura feared to listen to the purport of her speech, lest the manner and the matter united should prove too much for her gravity; and rising, she apologised for retiring, by saying, that she heard her father stir, and that she must attend him.

Self-Control (1811)

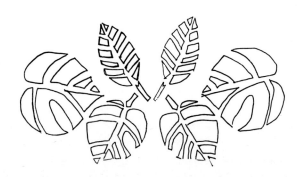

A LETTER FROM NORTH RONALDSAY

IAN SCOTT

(Ian Scott is one of the most talented artists of his generation, his sculpture and paintings and drawings having been exhibited widely, but much of his creative time in his native island of North Ronaldsay where he farms and fishes is spent in shaping not stone and metal, but the ongoing life of the community, through activities which include the annual Harvest Home, held in the old hall amongst greenery and candlelight. In reports to the local press he portrays the life of an island and its people and its background of the sea.)

This is Sunday, August 16, and as I write the sun will, in a few minutes before 9 pm, disappear beneath a pale blue sea. Outside my west-facing window there is a glorious fuchsia tree festooned with countless flowers of the deepest and richest red, showing up beautifully against the dark green of the leaves, and in the still air bees are humming away as they work among this treasure trove of red and purple flowers. Above the old tree and a fragrant honeysuckle, myriads of small flies are dancing in endless patterns of up and down flight, and far away beyond their domain, a few clouds are slowly drifting across the sky, their edges tinged an orangey yellow by the rays of the fast setting sun.

I am going to tell you about two memorable days which have been and gone on the island, the first of which was two days ago, and it was a marvellous experience of sun and clear blue skies. A few clouds appearing from time to time, were moved on by a cool wind blowing lightly from the north-west. That day's stream flood tides saw two good and lightsome pundings – one at Snaetin and another at Trindly. Many shears clicked away busily for a few hours.

Then in the late afternoon, after the heat of the day, a North Ronaldsay praam worked away, at times gliding over the sea, pale powder blue – like that wonderful colour of the starling's egg – which stretched away north and west as smooth as satin. Passing between Seal Skerry and the land, and moving east into deeper water, the boat jumped briefly in a minor blue-black tide fall before passing the tall banded tower of the North Ronaldsay lighthouse, which, as the praam moved swiftly on, looked for an instant to be almost cut in two by the blaze of the setting sun. All the time in the east, the moon was rising by degrees, and by degrees becoming brighter until, an hour or so later, her yellowish face reflected a wide path of light across the water – looking as if one of our great northern giants had thrown a cauldron of liquid gold towards the moon only to fall glittering upon the night sea. Once round Dennis Taing, with the path of gold following the boat, the darkening line of the island appeared, stretching north and south, with winking lights showing up here and there from silhouetted houses.

Changing my line of vision from this spectacular moonlit scene of sea, land, and sky, to the darkened tulfers of the boat, I chanced to see, in sudden and considerable contrast, a small sand eel, slim, silver-coloured, and quite exquisite.

Later, from a happy and busy Community Centre in the process of being redecorated, and where over the summer between 500 and 600 attendances had been recorded by the warden, three hundred balloons were being blown up and tied into attractive clusters. Shortly, they were carried down the old school brae towards the following night's venue, the Memorial Hall. Imagine for a moment such a sight. By this time a brilliant moon lit up the island and reflected brightly on the floating, bobbing balloons, their various colours still easily seen. A warm south wind kept them streaming and dancing away as we walked along. Then an Oyster Catcher called sharply as it winged past. To the west a slight land sea rumbled quietly away, its sound echoing over the night air.

So my second day arrived – Saturday, August 15. In a hall decorated with balloons, flowers, and evergreens, a great night unfolded. It was planned and introduced by this year's warden, Ingrid Tulloch. In only three days a concert was conceived, practised, and carried out with considerable style and dash. The two teachers, Liz and Trevor Baxter, along with others helping, had worked extremely hard to successfully achieve this. Trevor, playing guitar, accompanied 10 young folk made up of North Ronaldsay school pupils and some visiting children, who sang and mimed their way through a selection of songs with wonderful enjoyment and confidence. Then 20 performers appeared on stage, the additional 10 made up by students from the KGS, and one or two other holiday makers. All sang delightfully together before the older group gave an audience of between 70 and 80 a number of fine melodic songs with Trevor accompanying.

At the end of the concert the warden proposed a suitable vote of thanks before tea and a magnificent selection of homebakes and sandwiches were served. After those refreshments, and without a moment's delay, the dance began. Three accordion players, made up by Ronald Swanney, leading in fine fettle and style, and supported by Lottie and Ann Tulloch (plus drums) began playing for what was to be the last dance for the summer. Kathleen Scott and Ian Deyell acted as Masters of Ceremony in an atmosphere that must have borrowed something from the great days of the past. The quality and mood of the evening was enjoyed by young and old alike including a very spry lady from London, aged 98. Through the night an island couple in their seventies and early eighties took part in a Scotch Reel, and so the dance went on with great enjoyment until the early hours of a new day. Donations for the Community Association amounted to over £80.

Outside the hall, now dark and silent, the moon, just fading slightly on her west edge, lit up the scene, and threw shadows of a little parting company across the road. There below the star-spangled dome of the sky they 'discoursed' briefly for a time. Directly above the hall, Cassiopeia, or the lady of the chairs, could be seen. Further east the Seven Sisters glittered coldly, and in the north, most prominent of all the constellations, the Plough, dominated the heavens. For the first time some of the youngest of the star gazers were helped to pick out a great star of the northern hemisphere. They followed an imaginary line from the two pointers of the Plough upwards, there to connect with another line drawn from the Plough handle, and at the peak of the ensuing triangle is positioned this star – so very far away, but through time and from generation to generation, it will remain fixed for the next few thousand years, always pointing to the north. It is, of course, Polaris, or the Pole Star.

I am finishing this letter on Sunday while looking through our east-facing window. In the background, on tape, I can hear Trevor Elliot playing 'The Carnival is Over' which sounds rather sad. A few garden trees are being blown backwards and forwards by the remains of last night's south-east gale. Rain also lashed down in the blackness and fury of the night, and the sea today, in brilliant sunshine, seems to move in a living sweeping mass to the north. I am ever more aware that summer has been slipping away, as time is, bringing with its passing, inevitable changes. Trevor now plays the traditional old song 'A Bunch of Thyme,' and I feel there is little more I can say.

'Days to Remember', *The Orcadian* (August 1992)

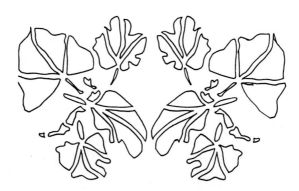

REMEMBERING GEORGE CORRIGALL

MARY BICHAN

(In the various concerts that were highlights of Orkney life in the 1950s, one of the most eagerly anticipated moments was always the appearance on stage of George Corrigall. On he would come, to loud applause, radiating enjoyment and good humour. Many of his songs have become classics, and the more you hear them, the more you realise how beautifully-crafted they were. When Radio Orkney decided to present a series looking back on George Corrigall, the ideal person to script it was Mary Bichan. Mary lives in the same parish of Harray, at the farm of Caperhouse with her husband, and over the years she has been involved in many concerts and community activities. Today she is Orkney Islands Councillor for Harray and Stenness. This is from the first of her programmes, in 1981.)

It's twenty years since George Corrigall died, at the age of 57. It seems strange that anyone under the age of 30 will have no memory of him at all, and may have difficulty in realising just how popular an entertainer he was at concerts and social gatherings of all kinds. Set to popular tunes, his verses dealt with many topical local subjects and people.

George was born in December 1904, and lived all his life at West Ballarat in Harray. I don't think that a better description of him could be given than that by author Garry Hogg in his book *The Far-Flung Isles*, in which he says:

At a croft at West Ballarat, overlooking the loch, we found a small neat man of fifty-odd, in heavy tweed trousers and hand-knitted pullover of deepish purple, shifting muck in a wheel-barrow. 'George Corrigall?' 'That's me,' he answered, putting down his barrow to shake hands with us, 'Come awa in.'

That was indeed typical of the way George welcomed everyone, no matter how busy he was.

He started his public appearances in Harray, so I think it appropriate that we should start with a song that was tremendously popular in the parish. Folk never tired of hearing it. This was 'Strolling up the Lyde.'

The Lyde is the valley between Harray and Rendall, and before the days of the motor-car it was a favourite walk or cycle run for courting couples. There is a reference to a local landmark that can still be seen; that is the pump at the Harray end of the Lyde, which is on the property of Cribbaquoy, occupied in George's time by Edward Irvine.

One of the Russian leaders of the time was Mr Vishinsky, which is not an easy name to fit into an Orkney song. But George manages it, and suggests an admirable cure for his uncooperative obstinacy.

Strolling up the Lyde!

BBC Radio Orkney recording, May 7th 1981

STROLLING UP THE LYDE

GEORGE CORRIGALL

(Tune: 'Sailing down the Clyde')

Oh, the world may think of its wondrous roads
   In countries far away
Like the Burma Road or the Pekin Road
   Or the Road to Mandalay,
But we the most romantic road
   Where fragrant memories cling
And Harray men both aald and young
   Will join with me and sing –

Strolling up the Lyde, with your lassie by your side,
Such a bonny lassie, she's your joy and pride,
Looking forward to the day when she'll be your bonny bride
And you'll settle down togetehr at your ain fireside.

Oh, the Harray folks are a jolly lot
   When the storms of winter roar,
They've a grand community centre noo
   With games and fun galore,
Dramatics, darts and badminton,
   And they play them with a will,
And the menfolk aal agree with me
   That it's even finer still –

When you're strolling up the Lyde, with your lassie by your side,
That's the trip that fills your head with joy and pride,
Looking forward to the day when she'll be your bonny bride
And you'll settle down together at your ain fireside.

Noo it seems to me that the world's affairs
  Are in a dreadful plight
Vishinsky's such a stubborn chap,
  And nothing's going right.
Noo I think it would even cure
  Vishinsky of the dumps
If he would meet a Harray lass
  At Edward Irvine's pump –

And go strolling up the Lyde, with the lassie by his side
It would fill his poor owld grumpy hairt with joy and pride;
He'd be such a happy man, that on peace he would decide,
And mankind would live contented at their ain fireside.

THE APPROACH OF WINTER

ELAINE R. BULLARD

November treated Orkney kindly. For once no gales swept summer into winter without pause for autumn tints. On the last Sunday afternoon of the month I visited a peaty hill near the sea where a burn, no more than a pace in width, has made for itself a miniature rocky gorge.

Here were russet of rare bracken and frosted docken, red of cotton grass, yellows of leaves of primrose and tormentil, while those still clinging to stiff stalks of meadow-sweet were crumpled brown and pale beige. Heather and woodrush were not yet bleached to cold grey by salt-laden winds. Between the roots of these were many kinds of moss; some had ferny fronds, others were cushion-deep, and a handful of sphagnum left a creamy white hole, like biting into a green-skinned apple. An otter's track tunnelled through the tangled purple twigs of dwarf willow.

Above Scotland the clouds had taken the last of the sunset but overhead the clearer sky was flecked with pink. Scapa Flow had the dull gleam of new unpolished lead, and floating seabirds were dark silhouettes. It was very still and even a wren forgot to scold.

These calm days in Orkney are precious. Too soon the light faded and car headlights shone on the Orphir road. It was four o' clock.

Manchester Guardian Weekly, December 11th 1958.

MERLIN

EDWIN MUIR

(To round off, who better than Edwin Muir? Introducing his Collected Poems in 1965, T. S. Eliot said that he would 'remain among the poets who have added glory to the English language.' Muir, he said, had in particular 'one very rare and precious quality' – he was a man 'of complete integrity.' Born in Deerness in 1887 – the same year as Stanley Cursiter – Edwin Muir and his family stayed some years at the Bu in Wyre. He had to live through hard times, in the struggle to survive when they moved to Glasgow, and also in the havoc and destruction which he witnessed descending on Europe in the years of dictatorship, oppression and war, to places like Dresden, Hellerau and Prague, where he and his wife Willa had lived. But out of it all came a deep and compassionate poetic vision.)

O Merlin in your crystal cave
Deep in the diamond of the day,
Will there ever be a singer
Whose music will smooth away
The furrow drawn by Adam's finger
Across the meadow and the wave?

Or a runner who'll outrun
Man's long shadow driving on,
Break through the gate of memory
And hang the apple on the tree?
Will your magic ever show
The sleeping bride shut in her bower,
The day wreathed in its mound of snow
And Time locked in his tower?

Journeys and Places (1937)